The
GROW YOUR OWN FOOD
Handbook

The
GROW YOUR OWN FOOD
Handbook

A BACK TO BASICS GUIDE TO PLANTING, GROWING, AND HARVESTING FRUITS AND VEGETABLES

MONTE BURCH

Skyhorse Publishing

Skyhorse Publishing books may be purchased in bulk at special discounts for sales promotion, corporate gifts, fund-raising, or educational purposes. Special editions can also be created to specifications. For details, contact the Special Sales Department, Skyhorse Publishing, 307 West 36th Street, 11th Floor, New York, NY 10018 or info@skyhorsepublishing.com.

Skyhorse® and Skyhorse Publishing® are registered trademarks of Skyhorse Publishing, Inc.®, a Delaware corporation.

www.skyhorsepublishing.com

10 9 8 7 6

Library of Congress Cataloging-in-Publication Data is available on file.
ISBN: 978-1-62873-803-2

Printed in China

Contents

The
GROW YOUR OWN FOOD
Handbook

1

Why Grow Your Own Food

Learning to grow food was a milestone in the development of the human race. As hunters and gatherers learned to cultivate food, they began to develop societies. Many of the Native Americans were expert food growers and taught the pilgrims to grow native foods such as corn, beans, and squash, thus sustaining the struggling settlements. A community food garden was the norm as these settlements grew. As the pioneers worked their way across the country, a food garden was a necessity for survival. In days past, every farm had a big garden, and even

⟪ Growing your own food offers many benefits including a reduced use of our dwindling energy supplies as food is processed, packaged, and shipped all over the world.

those in the cities with big backyards grew their own food. These days a much smaller number of people grow their own food, while most depend on the grocery-store shelves to provide their nutrition.

These days, with all of our purchased food, we expect foods not in season to be available year-round. We also enjoy the experience of tasting new foods that have never been available in our local areas. This convenience comes at a high cost. Transporting food from east to west and from north to south from one end of the country to the other and from one country to another is a major use of oil for fuel. Packaging foods to be shipped also utilizes a tremendous amount of energy, as well as oil for producing plastic and trees for paper. Other major factors, however, are the taste and texture of food. Much of the produce found on today's grocery-store shelves is bred to be picked green, not ripe, so it won't ripen before it hits the stores. This produces, in some instances, a tasteless, hard-textured food. Just compare the hot-house tomato to a juicy freshly picked tomato from the garden.

So why grow your own food? Granted, we can't all have huge gardens completely fulfilling our food needs. But there are several good reasons to grow what we can. First is the taste. You simply can't beat the taste of freshly picked sweet corn, brought in from the garden and directly to the table. The taste of homegrown tomatoes, ripe and bursting with juice, is heaven to a tomato lover. And how about fresh green beans with new potatoes, one of our family's favorite homegrown dishes. Even those with limited space can grow their own salad garden, with fresh lettuce, spinach, onions, and radishes. Peaches and apples, luscious blueberries, blackberries, and strawberries that taste nothing like store-bought ones are also prime foods you can grow.

The second reason is health. More and more problems are developing with commercially grown and processed foods. By growing your own, you can limit the use of harmful chemicals such as pesticides, insecticides, and herbicides. Or you may decide not to use any chemicals and grow organically. You will know what your family is eating when you grow it yourself. Doctors and researchers

❮ Tasting your own ripe tomatoes, fresh green beans, blueberries, and peaches, as well as apricots off your own trees, is far different from the produce you find at your local grocer's.

❯ For many, attaining good health is the reason for growing their own food. By growing your own foods, you can control what's used in the way of pesticides and other chemicals, as well as fertilizers. The cabbage shown has a few chewed insect holes, but no chemicals.

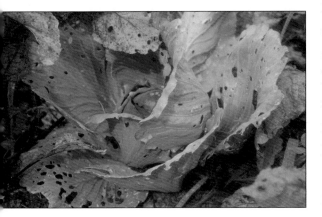

warn of our growing health problems from diabetes and obesity. Many people, especially youngsters, live on fast foods and don't even get a minimum daily requirement of fruits and vegetables. Health.gov suggests we need two to three servings of fruits and vegetables each day. Most fruits and vegetables are low in calories and high in vitamins and fiber. Growing your own fruits and vegetables increases the opportunity for more healthy foods for your family.

The third reason is also health related. Growing your own food gets you outside and serves as a form of exercise. Although too much sun can be dangerous, studies have shown a lack of sunlight to be a common problem with many people. Fresh air, sunlight, and enjoying the outdoors are also stress relievers. Tilling, planting, weeding, watering, and harvesting all require effort, creating healthy daily exercises.

The fourth reason is simply economics. You can definitely save money growing your own food. And if you grow enough to put food up for future use either by canning, drying, root-cellaring, or freezing, the savings really mount up. We always keep a record of what we grow, eat, and put up each year. It doesn't, however, count what we eat fresh as well as the bushels of produce and fruit we give away to neighbors, friends, and family. The amount and types of food varies from year to year. For instance, one year we might have an abundance of sweet corn but fewer tomatoes, or lots of broccoli one year followed by a less-productive year. Our orchard often overproduces, followed by a year with little or no fruit. When we have an abundance of fruit, everyone gets jams and jellies for Christmas. The following is our record for 2010 and the month the food was put up.

⊗ Homegrown fruits and vegetables are just plain good for you.

May, 2 pt. spinach (freezer)
May, 4 pt. asparagus (freezer)
May, 4 pt. spinach (freezer)
June, 3½ gal. chopped apricots for
    jam (freezer)
June, 7 qt. apricot halves in light
    syrup (pie filling/freezer)
June, 1 gal. sugar snap peas
    (loose-frozen)
June, 4 qt. strawberries (freezer)
June, 8 qt. apricot halves (freezer)
June, 3 qt. dried apricot halves
June, 6 qt. raspberries (freezer)
June, 2 qt. asparagus (freezer)

⊗ Growing your own food is a major step in saving money — and if you process the foods you grow, you really save.

June, 8 qt. blueberries (freezer)

June, 3 batches apricot jam

June, 1 gal. apricot halves for cobbler (freezer)

June, 2 batches apricot jam

June, 4 qt. strawberries (freezer)

June, 2 qt. rhubarb (freezer)

June, 2 qt. asparagus (freezer)

June, 6 qt. chopped cabbage (freezer)

July, 2 qt. French-cut green beans (freezer)

July, 14 qt. green beans (pressure canned)

July, 7 qt. beets (pressure canned)

July, 14 pt. beet pickles (pressure canned)

July, 14 qt. green beans (pressure canned)

July, 14 qt. sweet corn, cut off the cob (freezer)

July, 4 qt. and 6 pt. blackberries (freezer)

July, 4 qt. rhubarb (freezer)

July, 7 qt. sweet dill pickles (water bath canned)

July, 7 qt. whole tomatoes (pressure canned)

August, 7 qt. sweet sliced pickles (water bath canned)

August, 2 gal. refrigerator dill pickles

August, 9 pt. tomato and onion concentrate (freezer)

August, 7 qt. whole plum tomatoes (pressure canned)

August, 4 qt. strawberries (freezer)

August, 2 qt. peaches (freezer)

August, 4 qt. zucchini (freezer)

August, 13 pt. tomato relish (pressure canned)

August, 11 pt. hot salsa (pressure canned)

August, 13 pt. mild salsa (pressure canned)

August, 5 bushels potatoes (basement cellar)

August, 14 qt. peach halves (pressure canned)

August, 7 pt. tomato and onion concentrate (freezer)

August, 3 qt. peaches (freezer)

August, 2 gal. peaches for cobbler (freezer)

August, 2 qt. peaches (freezer)

August, 2 gal. peaches for cobbler (freezer)

August, 14 pt. Italian-flavored plum tomatoes (pressure canned)

August, 3 gal. peaches for cobbler (freezer)

August, 14 pt. taco sauce (pressure canned)

August, 6 pt. cantaloupe in light syrup (freezer)

August, 7 qt. pizza sauce mix with three meats (freezer)

September, 9 pt. pears (pressure canned)

September, 16 pt. apple butter (water bath canned)

September, 32 qt. tomato juice (pressure canned)

September, 2 qt. fried apples, ready to heat and serve (freezer)

September, 4 pans apple-pie filling (freezer)

September, 2 qt. apple peels for jelly (extra peels make a rosy red apple jelly, freezer)

September, 7 pt. tomato-and-onion concentrate (freezer)

October, 7 pt. roasted red bell peppers (freezer)

October, 6 pans stuffed peppers, ready to cook (freezer)

October, 10 pt. roasted red bell peppers (freezer)

October, 5 qt. bags sweet (red, green, and yellow) peppers, diced (freezer)

October, 4 qt. bags sweet (red, green, and yellow) peppers, diced (freezer)

October, 6 qt. fried apples, ready to heat and serve (freezer)

October, 6 qt. bags sweet peppers, diced (freezer)

October, 6 bushels sweet potatoes (basement cellar)

October, 4 cups grated horseradish

October, 7 pt. roasted red, green, and yellow peppers, diced (freezer)

October, 6 qt. bags sweet red and green peppers, diced (freezer)

As of October 2010, apples were still available as well as a freezer of strawberries, raspberries, and blackberries to be made into jams and jellies. A bushel of green tomatoes is slowly ripening in the garage and will provide ripe tomatoes through Thanksgiving. I'm not sure I can even figure how much money we have saved this year growing our own food. If you take the green beans and beets alone and figure ¢75 a can, two cans or $1.50 per quart, at 44 quarts, that's $66.00. Our cost for seed and fertilizer for that same produce was less than $10.00. When you begin to figure the savings in fruit, you really save, especially fruit ready to serve.

Granted not everyone has the time, inclination, and space to grow and put up this quantity of food, but any amount you grow yourself is a help.

If you can't grow your own food, or are limited in what you can grow, a major step you can take is to purchase from farmers' markets and other local sources. Not only are you "greening" by cutting down on the use of fuel for transportation, but you are also enjoying much tastier and healthier foods. And you're helping the local economy.

2

Planning to Grow

Once you've decided to grow your own food, the next step is to plan your food garden. Planning is extremely important. The more time you spend planning, the fewer hassles you'll have, the more you will enjoy growing your own food, and the more productive it will be. The first step is to choose a location, the second is to decide what you want to grow, and the third is to decide how big a garden you want to have or how much you want to grow. It's important to be realistic in all three choices.

❰❰ Growing your own food requires a well-drained garden spot, with at least 6 to 8 hours of full sun per day.

Location

As with real estate, and a garden is "real estate," it's all about location, location, location. Most of us don't buy a home or purchase a property with a garden site foremost in mind. We're often limited to what's available. That's not to say with a little effort and imagination you can't grow most foods just about anywhere. Regardless of where you live, it's important to pick your best garden location depending on several factors. Understand your geographic area; the average mean temperatures, including first and last frosts; amount of sunlight; and the soil types. Elevation can have a great deal to do with frosts. We live on an Ozark hillside, but a good portion of our farm is down the hill in a valley, as are some of our neighbors, less than a quarter a mile away. We often don't get nearly as much frost as our neighbors or the valley below. Not only can we garden longer, but we also have better chances than our neighbors do for fruit blossom survival.

Folks in the north, with extremely short seasons and relatively cool weather, may have trouble growing long-season plants, although many northerners have discovered tricks for extending their season. Gardeners in those areas often grow plants started in row covers or cold frames to extend the season. The chapter on fall gardening covers many ideas on how you can extend your season, even grow foods year-round in some instances. On the other hand, growers in northern areas can grow rhubarb while those in the south have problems with this plant.

Sunlight is extremely important. Most vegetables, fruits, berries, and trees need full sun or at least six hours of full sun per day. This may require shade-tree pruning or even removal of a tree or two near your garden site. I had this problem for many years with an old oak on the west end of my garden, and I finally had to remove it. You can also build reflectors, including decorative fences, to help distribute more sunlight. Limited shading, however, is good for some plants. If possible, the garden should run south to north. This provides the optimum amount of sunlight as the sun travels east to west. If your garden runs east to west as does my current garden, you can remedy this by planting taller plants on the north and working south with shorter plants.

Try to locate the garden on a relatively level area, but in a place that drains well. If you have a slight slope, run the rows across the slope rather than up and down to prevent erosion. Severe slopes will require terracing. If the garden area doesn't drain well, as evidenced by continued puddles, you may need to utilize drain lines or, better yet, create raised beds. The garden should also be relatively close to a water source, in most cases a hose-supply faucet.

The next major factor is soil. Again this can vary, but in most instances, a garden plot isn't "ready-made" for productive food growing. As mentioned, a continually wet area is not a good spot. Extremely sandy soil causes other problems, as does a heavy-clay soil. Although we harvest a bountiful supply of food each year from our Ozark hillside garden, we probably have the worst garden spot. The topsoil is very thin. Dig about four inches down and you run into a hardpan of clay and

⊗ It's important to determine what types of and how much food you want to grow, as well as how much time you want to put into both growing and preserving.

flint stones. And there simply isn't a flat spot on our hillside home location. Our house starts at ground level in the front and ends up four feet above ground level at the back. And the garden location isn't much better. Two tactics have been used to create our productive food garden. The first was to terrace the hillside. We used logs cut from trimming our timberland, as well as railroad ties and landscaping timbers to build up the low side. Then came filling in the low area with good topsoil. Even that has been continually improved with regular additions of compost and well-rotted manure. We still continually till or dig up and garden around rocks, and we sometimes think the garden grows rocks better than anything else. Regardless, the soil produces.

What and How Much to Grow

This is the hard part for beginning food growers. Beginners usually want to grow everything, and you can grow almost any food you can buy. You should aim to produce as much high-quality food as possible from your growing area. Grow family favorites and a variety of foods so you can keep meals interesting and nutritious. It's also important to choose foods based on what you and your family like to eat. For instance, if no one will eat broccoli, why grow it?

Even if you have unlimited space, don't plan too large a garden, especially if you're new to gardening. It's best to have a well-kept small garden than a large garden that becomes too much work. I've been there. Years ago, when our kids were growing up, we had four gardens, a half-acre sweet corn patch, and a garden just for potatoes. One year the potato patch produced a pickup truck load of potatoes. Then there was the general-purpose garden and finally a garden for the wildlife. We all worked long days from light to dark to grow our food. These days my wife and I have only one garden, and it's not particularly big; we're just growing "smarter." Sorry for the pun. The garden is better organized, utilizes a lot of raised beds, and is about one-fourth the work, yet produces an abundance of food. Growing some plants in volume in the home garden isn't practical, except for the satisfaction of growing food and the fun of tasting your own homegrown

produce. Specific plants require specific spacing, depending on whether they are grown in conventional rows or intensive gardening. Chapter 6 on "Vegetable Specifics" illustrates how much food can be grown in specific spacing, as well as how much is needed per person. Measure your garden area to determine how much space is available. Some plants can be grown in small spaces; others, such as corn and potatoes, require larger areas. After determining how much space you have and how much your garden can theoretically produce, the next step is to consider realistically how much time and effort you want to put into growing and processing your own food. Growing your own food can be time-consuming, especially if you grow enough to process or store for future use. There's the garden preparation: seeding and planting, weeding, watering, harvesting, and processing. The latter can also be a lot of work. An example of the time involved is our sweet corn patch. We've harvested enough roasting ears in one weekend to last us for thirty days in the refrigerator, plus put numerous quarts of cut-off-the-cob corn in the freezer. Not counting the time involved in planting

and maintaining, it takes my wife Joan and I one whole weekend to shuck, process, and store the harvest. Other plants aren't quite so much work. We dug almost two hundred pounds of sweet potatoes from six plants and simply stored them in the basement. Some plants also require more effort in growing, and again corn is one of those, although with some tricks and techniques, you can cut down on a lot of the work. Some of the easiest vegetables to grow in volume, however, include corn, as well as potatoes, bush beans, cabbage, tomatoes, lettuce, spinach, and other salad greens.

Other plants do not produce the quantity but still have a place in your garden simply because the homegrown foods taste so good. A good example of this is peas. We grow peas simply because they taste so great with new potatoes in the spring, but we've found it hard to grow, harvest, and pod more than a few pints for the freezer. Green beans, on the other hand, often become so prolific it's hard to keep up with the volume, and we pressure can lots of beans, eat lots, and give away lots. It does, however, take time to snap and process any volume of green beans. Some plants, fifty pounds of delicious, mouth-watering homegrown tomatoes each season. By all means, include some tomatoes in your garden. Beans, broccoli, cabbage, lettuce, zucchini squash, chard, and spinach are all plants that produce a lot of food in limited areas.

Before you begin to plant your garden, plan it on paper. Use a tape measure or step off to measure the size of your food plot. Again, chapter 6 details the spacing of specific plants in a traditional row garden, as well as how many plants are normally needed per person. Using this you can lay out your garden on paper. Use squared or drafting paper, or mark off squares on paper with a ruler, with each square representing one foot. Then write in where you want to position different food plants.

Also, remember you don't have to grow all your food at one time; successive plantings can keep your garden producing throughout the growing season. Plan your garden to take advantage of fences that might be bordering it, for instance growing peas, cucumber, or pole beans on the fences. Most importantly, however, is positioning plants so tall-growing

⊗ Some plants require more space than others. A lot of tomatoes can be grown in a small space.

such as corn and watermelons, take a lot of space to grow. Tomatoes also take up space, but grown vertically, they take up less space and are a garden favorite. One tomato plant, grown properly, can produce up to

Burch 2010 Garden Plan

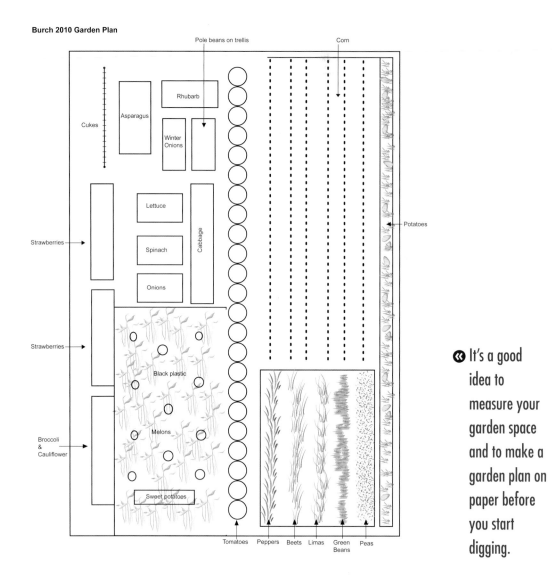

> ⊗ It's a good idea to measure your garden space and to make a garden plan on paper before you start digging.

plants don't shade out shorter plants. If a garden runs east to west, for example, corn and pole beans should be planted on the north side, followed by tomato plants in cages, then beans and potatoes, followed by lettuce and other lower-growing plants. Living in a rural area and with a big yard, we've always grown the traditional big farm garden, although we've scaled back greatly in the past few years. Our present garden runs east to west, measures 30 × 50 feet, and one-fourth of the garden is completely made of raised beds. Three of the beds contain strawberries, with

Diary Tomato Varieties

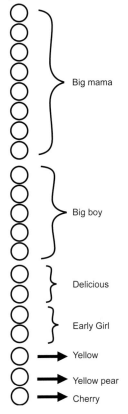

Big mama

Big boy

Delicious

Early Girl

Yellow

Yellow pear

Cherry

◉ Keep a diary with a sketch or plan of what varieties are planted. Also note how each variety grew and produced in that given year. Over the years this diary will become invaluable in choosing varieties that thrive in your garden.

the bed portion. One-half of the bed portion is used to grow lettuce, cabbage, broccoli, cucumbers, squash, spinach, radishes, onions, and other salad greens. The other half of the bed portion, or one-fourth of the garden, is used to grow watermelons, cantaloupe, muskmelons, and honeydew melons, along with a plant or two of pumpkins.

Some plants do better with their crops rotated each year, so remember to keep your garden plans from year to year in order to determine crop rotations. We also make up a planting plan as well for crops such as tomatoes and peppers, where more than one variety is often planted in a row or bed. This lists each variety planted so we can determine which varieties do best each year. Keep a diary of what grew best, how long it took plants to germinate or fruit, the weather conditions, and the first and last frosts. These paper records will become invaluable over the years. If you put up or give away surplus foods, keep a record of that as well.

Interplant species that can be grown together with some maturing faster than their companion plants. For instance, plant radishes and

one bed rejuvenated every year so we can keep a continuous supply of plants going. The regular-row portion is used to grow corn, beans, and potatoes. A single row of tomato cages and a half row of tomatoes and half row of peppers divide the row portion from

⊗ Interplanting slow- and fast-growing varieties, such as spinach, radishes, and onions to be used as young green onions, produces the most from your growing space.

carrots together. As you harvest the radishes, the slower-growing carrots will have more room to grow and are automatically "thinned." Another tactic to produce a longer salad garden is to grow varieties of lettuce that grow well in cool weather but tend to bolt in hot weather. Follow this with New Zealand spinach that can produce salad greens even in hot weather.

Save one spot in the garden for trying new varieties or even new species each year. It adds to the fun of growing your own food and also spices up your meals.

While planning your garden, make the most of local gardeners. Most are more than delighted to discuss their food gardens. Check out local county extension offices for information. Good information on what grows best in your area is available and will save you a lot of time, expense, and hassle. Part of the fun of growing your own food is poring over the various seed catalogs and drooling over the mouth-watering photos of delicious foods. These catalogs can also be a great help in planning your garden. In many instances, more varieties of seed are available earlier than can be found locally. Other seeds—such as corn, spinach, beets, lettuce, and onion sets—or plants are more economical if purchased in bulk locally and are available when it's time to plant.

With time spent planning your food garden, you'll enjoy a productive, money-saving, tasty supply of food for you, your family, and probably even some of your friends.

3

Preparing the Site

Growing your own food requires more than simply throwing out some seeds. You will need to create a growing area. Preparing the growing site can be a great deal of work, or relatively easy depending on the site location, soil type, and whether or not a garden has already existed on the area. No matter what type of soil the site has, it can probably be improved. The very first essential step is to take a soil test. Remove the sod and dig up several samples of soil from the area. Mix these samples together in a plastic container and allow them to dry. Take a half pint of the sample to your local cooperative extension

 Properly preparing the growing site is vital for a productive garden such as this garden with tomatoes, corn, and green beans.

office. It will take about a week for the sample to be sent to the test center and will cost just a few bucks. The results of the soil sample will tell you what materials you will need to add to your soil.

Understanding Soil

A short "science class" can help in understanding your soil and how to create a productive food garden. First, soil is the single most important ingredient of any garden. Second, soil is alive and constantly changing. Third, any soil can be improved. Fourth, all garden soils need regular maintenance and care. One of the most important factors in soil is the size and arrangement of the particles. This determines the type of soil and how you can amend it. A simple demonstration can provide you with the type of soil in your garden location. Place a quarter cup of soil from your garden location and a pint of water in a glass fruit jar. Place a lid or cap on the jar and shake well. Allow the particles to settle for a few minutes and then shake well again. Set the jar aside for five to seven days. The soil will settle out

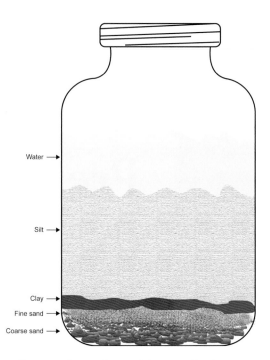

Water →
Silt →
Clay →
Fine sand →
Coarse sand →

⊘ You must first understand the type of soil in your garden site. A soil sample placed in a jar of water will settle out, providing a description of your type of soil.

in layers, and the water will clear. Study the different layers in the jar. The heaviest particles, coarse sand or small rocks, will make up the bottom layer, followed by fine sand, then silt, and finally clay. Bits of organic matter may also be floating on top of the water. If the sediment is half sand, it is called a light sandy soil. If the sediment is over half silt but with little clay, it's called a heavy silt soil. If it is more than one-fourth clay with a large amount of silt, it's called a clay soil. If the layers are about two-fifths sand, two-fifths silt, and the rest clay, it's called a good loam, the ideal soil.

Each of these soil types has pluses and minuses. A light sandy soil is easy to work, warms up quickly in the spring, and normally has good drainage. It, however, won't hold moisture or nutrients very long, so it needs water and fertilizer more often. Adding organic matter, peat moss, compost, leaf mold, or sawdust can help the soil retain moisture and nutrients. Heavy clay or silt soils are slower to warm and dry out in the spring, usually drain poorly, and compact very easily. They shouldn't be worked when wet, or they will form hard clumps or clods. Add organic matter to make them lighter and more porous. Adding quantities of coarse but not light sand can also help.

Humus is a very important part of soil. Humus is basically the result of decomposition, actually the "life" of the soil. It's just about impossible for a soil to have too much humus, and most soils don't have nearly enough. Humus adds a number of the nutrients soil needs and improves the texture or tilth of the soil, allowing it to better absorb and hold water and nutrients. Humus also acts as a buffer against the problems of possible overdoses of fertilizer and, in some cases, some herbicides. Rich, deep, well-fertilized soil that is dark brown or black is often called a humus soil.

Humus is an organic matter, produced by countless microorganisms that break down dead tissues and then reduce them further into chemical forms plants can utilize. Humus is constantly being lost and replaced in nature. In gardening or farming, more humus is normally lost than is naturally replaced. For this reason, you should always add humus of some sort when you prepare a garden to plant. This humus can be compost, manure, peat moss, leaf mold, and other organic materials. Compost is the best choice, as the organic materials added directly to the soil and dug in can create a temporary nitrogen deficiency. If you dig undecayed organic materials into the soil, add a bit of nitrogen. A green manure crop can also add humus. Ryegrass or clover is plowed under after it is about half grown. Normally this is done by planting in the fall and plowing under in the spring.

Making Compost

The single most important chore you can do to grow a lot of food is to add compost to your garden site. Compost is basically made up of organic materials that have already been broken down or are in the last steps of being broken down by microorganisms. Mother Nature does this naturally when plants, insects, and animals die, returning them to the soil. The soil organisms decompose the organic matter so their nutrients can be used by plants. Decomposing is going on all the time all around us. Composting basically organizes and speeds up the process. Many communities now ban waste such as grass clippings, leaves, paper, and other natural materials from public landfills and are composting them instead. Do-it-yourself composting will greatly improve your food garden while recycling materials from your yard and kitchen. Composting is easy, and when done properly, it doesn't provide noxious smells nor create a "nuisance" appearance. Basically all you need to do is toss grass clippings, leaves, and even your coffee grounds into a bin, and in about four weeks or less, you'll have free fertilizer to add to your soil. In most instances, composting is done in a bin that can be made fairly inexpensively from a number of materials—stacked concrete blocks, a cage of welded wire, chicken wire, old hay bales, even landscaping timbers, or a constructed wooden bin. The latter is fairly easy to make even for a non-do-it-yourselfer. Regardless of the material used, the bin should have lots of holes for air circulation. The bin should be able to hold a pile of materials about three feet square and three feet high. Any smaller and it won't work quite as efficiently; any taller and the materials

❽ Compost is the single most important material you can add to any growing site. It's easy to create, as well as a great way of recycling materials from your yard and kitchen. A compost bin can be made quite easily using treated 5/4-inch decking boards.

Compost bin all treated wood

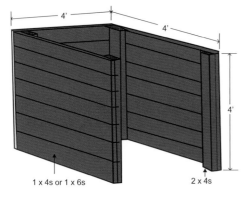

4'   4'   4'

1 x 4s or 1 x 6s   2 x 4s

may compact rather than stay loose for proper composting.

The first step is to choose a site that's well drained and on bare soil. If possible, locate the bin close to your garden to avoid hauling. The bin should be in a partially shady area to prevent direct sunlight from drying the materials out too quickly. The north side of a building is an ideal location. You should also be able to reach the bin with a garden hose. Many gardeners like to build two bins, one that's "working" and one that holds finished compost. The two bins are used together, tossing materials back and fourth. Three bins work even better, with two bins working and one holding materials to be composted.

Although you can simply dump materials into the bin, the best method is to divide the organic materials into two categories: dry or brown materials, which are high in carbon, and green or wet materials, which are high in nitrogen. The dry materials include straw, wood chips, dried leaves, and dried plants. The green materials include grass clippings and green leaves, as well as manure, green garden waste, and kitchen scraps. Do not use meat scraps, fat, or other foods

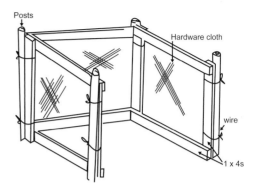

Another easy compost bin can be made from 1 x 4s and hardware cloth.

that will attract the neighborhood critters. Experts like to divide the two materials into about twenty-five to thirty parts high-carbon materials and one part high-nitrogen materials. Shred or cut up larger materials as much as possible. Use a lawn mower to chop leaves and cut kitchen scraps and garden refuse as small as possible or blend with a bit of water. The smaller the size of the materials, the more their surface is exposed, and the quicker the pile will decompose. Do not add weeds that have seed heads. Also, be aware some herbicides can remain in the plants and kill plants when used as compost.

Then it's simply a matter of placing the materials in the bin in layers. Start with a four-to-five-inch layer of coarse brown matter. Add a thin layer of green materials such as grass clippings, manure, and so forth. Add about a one inch layer of garden soil. This will help introduce the microorganisms needed for composting. Then add more brown materials such as dried hay, straw, or leaves. Follow with a thin layer of green materials. Sprinkle with water as you build up the layers. Build the pile to at least three feet high. Once you have the pile constructed, cover with a tarp or old piece of plywood to keep rainwater from slowing the composting process. An ideal bin has a cover constructed to fit.

Allow the pile to sit for a couple of days and then, using a pitchfork, turn the pile. This is where the second bin comes in. It's easier to simply fork the pile into the second bin than turn over all the materials in one bin. Turn the top, bottom, and sides of the pile into the center. This introduces air into the pile and exposes fly eggs and plant pathogens to the heat created by the decomposing pile. Turn and mix the pile at least every third day. Turning it more often will speed up the process. If the pile has been properly made and turned, it will heat up in a few days to approximately 160°F in the center. The pile will return to this temperature each time it is turned until

Layering Compost

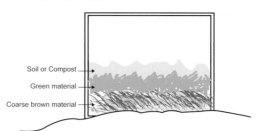

Soil or Compost
Green material
Coarse brown material

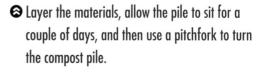

⊗ Layer the materials, allow the pile to sit for a couple of days, and then use a pitchfork to turn the compost pile.

it eventually begins to cool down. After about three or four weeks, the pile will cool down completely, and the materials can then be added to the garden. You really don't have to create a big compost pile. Compost can actually be created in any number of small compost makers available through garden-supply catalogs. Or simply place materials in large plastic leaf bags with holes punched in them. Dampen the materials in the bags and place in an out-of-the-way place. Turn and shake the bags twice a week, and you should have compost in a couple of months.

Fertilizer

Even with the addition of humus and compost, to maintain good soil fertility, you will need to add some sort of fertilizer on a regular basis. Most organic materials are low in phosphate and produce limited amounts of nitrogen. Growing plants need nutrients, including the elements magnesium, phosphorus, potassium, and nitrogen. Magnesium (Mg) comes from limestone. The amount of magnesium carbonate in ground limestone varies quite a bit. Phosphorus (P) has many important functions in plants, the primary one being the storage and transfer of energy through the plant. Adenosine diphosphate (ADP) and adenosine triphosphate (ATP) are high-energy phosphate compounds that control most processes in plants, including photosynthesis, respiration, protein and nucleic acid synthesis, and nutrient transport through the cell walls. Phosphorus is essential for seed production, and it promotes increased root growth, produces healthy growth, and encourages good fruit development. Rock phosphate is the most common source of phosphorus.

Potassium (K) comes from muriate of potash, derived from large deposits of potassium chloride salts found in the southwestern desert

⊗ Each type of plant has different fertilizer requirements. For instance, corn requires fertilizer high in nitrogen.

⊗ Growing food requires some sort of regularly applied fertilizer. These may be commercially produced chemical fertilizers or organic, or a combination of both.

of the United States. Potassium is needed for the manufacture of carbohydrates—sugars and starches. Potassium also increases resistance to disease and produces strong plant cell walls and stems. Nitrogen (N) is necessary to convert the sun's light into energy through photosynthesis. Plants also use nitrogen to form amino acids, the building blocks of protein. The availability of usable nitrogen often determines the quality of plants. Plants with dark green leaves have a high or proper amount of nitrogen availability. Slow-growing, stunted plants or those with yellowing leaves show a nitrogen deficiency. Each plant has different nitrogen requirements. Corn, for instance, has one of the highest nitrogen requirements, needing as much as 215 pounds of nitrogen per acre to produce high yields. Legumes, such as clovers and beans, "fix" or add nitrogen to the soil. Rhizobium bacteria forms nodules on the roots of the plants and then takes nitrogen from the atmosphere and makes it available to the plants. For this reason, a cover crop of clover planted in late fall and tilled in late winter or early spring is a great way of

adding nitrogen to your food-growing site.

Different types of plants require different types of fertilizers. Chapter 6 on growing specific vegetables details the fertilizer requirements for each species. Fertilizers are available as chemical and as organic. The former are actually materials found growing naturally and ground or manufactured to produce nitrogen, phosphate, and potassium. The latter are from organic sources. Commercial chemical fertilizer is available in several forms. Farmers have a bulk fertilizer dealer mix the ingredients to specific requirements. For the small amounts needed, however, the most practical method for home food growers is to purchase bagged fertilizers. A numerical code on the bag indicates the amounts of each element. The first figure is the percent of N (nitrogen), the second is the percent of P (phosphate or phosphorus), and the third is the percent of K (potash or potassium). For example 8-31-16 has eight pounds of nitrogen, thirty-one pounds of phosphate, and sixteen pounds of potash per one hundred pounds. The rest of the materials are inert. The most common bagged commercial fertilizers are 10-10-10,

12-12-12, or 13-13-13. These contain all the elements in equal portions and are considered all-around general fertilizers. Simply applying these will provide the fertilizer requirements for most plants. Most vegetables, with exceptions like corn, are really not heavy feeders. Usually about five pounds of a general-purpose fertilizer should be applied to a one-hundred-foot square. Apply half the fertilizer before you prepare the soil and then add the remainder after the ground had been prepared, lightly raking the fertilizer into the top inch or so of soil. This positions fertilizer both for the seedlings when they first put down roots and deeper for when the plants begin to grow. Side-dressing with fertilizer also helps provide a maintenance supply of nutrients through the growing season.

Commercial garden fertilizers are also available. Many of these are designed specifically for plants such as beans, tomatoes, and so forth. Water-soluble gardening fertilizers designed to be applied with water, such as Miracle-Gro, are extremely easy to use. Dry commercial fertilizers can be overapplied, but the water-soluble fertilizers prevent that problem.

The water-soluble fertilizers can be applied by simply mixing a bit of the powder in a watering can, or with applicators holding the powder and fastened to a hose. The proper mix of fertilizer is applied as you water. This is a very consistent and easy way of adding fertilizer.

Organic fertilizers are the choice of many gardeners. The commercial fertilizers manufactured from rock and salt have a tendency to add salts to the soil, and many food growers prefer to utilize a more green approach. Different types of organic materials provide the different plant nutrient needs. The most common organic fertilizers are animal and bird manures. These are rated according to the nutrients, with rabbit manure the highest,

⊗ Commercial fertilizers are available in bagged (the most common) or in popular water-soluble forms.

❷ Different organic materials provide different elements of fertilizer.

Organic Fertilizer Chart (average percentage)			
Source	N	P	K
Alfalfa meal	2.50	.50	2.10
Blood meal	15.00	1.30	.70
Chicken manure (fresh)	1.63	1.54	.85
Clover hay	.55	.13	.50
Cow manure (fresh)	.29	.17	.35
Coffee grounds	1.99	.36	.68
Cotton seed meal	7.00	2.50	1.50
Fish meal	7.00	13.00	3.80
Greensand	.00	1.50	5.00
Horse manure (fresh)	.44	.18	.35
Oak leaves	.80	.35	.15
Rabbit manure (fresh)	1.80	1.65	.90
Seaweed	1.70	.75	5.00
Sheep manure (fresh)	.55	.31	.15
Wood ashes	.00	1.50	7.00

poultry manure or litter second, sheep manure third, horse fourth, and cow fifth. If you have a ready source of any of these manures, you're lucky. In most instances, you will need to purchase bagged manure, and it's usually cow manure that is available. All these manures also add humus or organic materials to the soil, helping to build the soil, the amount depending on the source. The manures also don't break down quite as rapidly as chemical fertilizers. Fresh manures should not be applied to the garden at planting time—especially poultry, rabbit, or horse manures—as they can burn the plants. The best tactic with fresh manure is to apply it in the fall or very early in the spring, plow it under, and then plant in the spring. Dried manure can be applied the same as with other fertilizers. One of the best ways of utilizing fresh manure is to compost it.

In addition to manure, other natural or organic materials can also supply the basic nutrients of nitrogen, phosphorus, and potash. These can be applied separately to match specific plant needs, or you can make up mixes that approximate commercial mixes. For instance, wood ashes contain phosphorus and potash, blood meal is high in nitrogen, and cottonseed meal contains fairly high amounts of nitrogen, phosphorus, and potash. Bone meal provides phosphorus. Most of these materials, however, are not readily available in bulk in most locales. The plant meals, such as cottonseed meal, are available, however, as they are often used as animal feeds and are available at farm and feed stores. Bone and blood meal may also be available in some areas. By using different quantities of the various available organic materials, you can make up general fertilizer mixes that resemble the amounts of elements in chemical fertilizers.

You can also make up your own liquid fertilizers using either fish or seaweed emulsion or manure. The latter, called manure tea, is easy to make and like other liquid fertilizers doesn't burn plants like some harsher fertilizers do. It does, of course, have a distinct smell. Since we live on a working cattle farm, with a cow-calf operation, we have lots of cow manure. We apply manure fresh and tilled in, use it dried to create humus and compost, and make our own manure tea. To make up your own manure tea, you'll need a five-gallon plastic bucket, a mesh bag, and, of course, dried cow manure. This can be purchased, or you may scoop your own. I guess you could utilize fresh manure, but believe me, dried is best. If you're not brave enough, you can make a compost tea, which isn't quite as "strong." Place the dried materials in a plastic bag that has holes in it. The ideal bag is one that is actually made of tightly woven plastic mesh. A pair of panty hose will also work. Place a rock in the bag for weight and tie the end shut. Place the bucket in a place where it won't collect rainwater and add the manure-filled bag. Fill the bucket with water. Place a board loosely over the bucket to keep out critters and allow the "tea" to steep for a few days. You can then pour off or dip the liquid and sprinkle over

⊗ You can make up your own manure tea liquid fertilizer.

Manure Tea

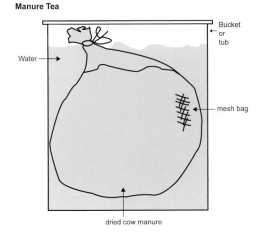

or around your plants with a garden watering can. You can add more water and steep another batch or two, but it gets weaker with time. I like to keep two buckets, one "working" and one finished to use as fertilizer.

Home food growers have the choice of using chemical or organic fertilizers for growing their food. This is a personal choice. Over time I've used both. Both types have advantages and disadvantages. Chemical fertilizers are quick and easy to use, and you can fertilize fairly precisely with them. You can, however, just as easily apply too much and burn or lose your crops. Chemical fertilizers are more costly (if you have access to the natural materials); they leach out of the soil fairly quickly and can run off into waterways, creating runoff problems. Over time the soil can also accumulate chemical salts, actually bringing down fertility or making it necessary to add continually more chemical fertilizers. For the most part, we've gotten away from chemical fertilizers on our farm operation and garden.

Organic fertilizers take a bit more time in applying, and they stay in the soil longer, but they will also leach from sandy soils. Organic gardening has become one of the green in things. In days past, organic gardeners

⊗ Some plants are heavy feeders; others are medium and others are only light feeders.

Fertilizer chart		
Heavy Feeders	*Medium Feeders*	*Light Feeders*
Asparagus	Broccoli	Bush beans
Cabbage (early)	Brussels sprouts	Beets
Cabbage (Chinese)	Cabbage (late)	Carrots
Cauliflower	Eggplant	Cucumbers
Corn	Lettuce	Peas
Onions	Peppers (small, hot)	Sweet potatoes
Peppers (large, sweet)	Potatoes (Irish)	Swiss chard
Rhubarb	Pumpkins	Tomatoes
Watermelon	Radishes	Turnips
	Spinach	

tended to use readily available bulk materials. With their new popularity, a lot of organic fertilizers are available commercially, even from the big-box stores. If you purchase small bags commercially, they can be costly. If you accumulate the materials in bulk, they're less expensive. The main advantage of organic fertilizers is they're basically recycling nature's materials, and their manufacture is not as hard on the environment. But most importantly, organic fertilizers, when used properly, have less chance of burning plants, and they add continual health to the soil in organic materials that decompose into the soil.

Different vegetables need different types of fertilizers. Plants such as corn and the leafy vegetables, such as lettuce, cabbage, kale, and spinach, require more nitrogen than other plants. Root and tuber crops, such as turnips, parsnips, carrots, beets, potatoes, and sweet potatoes, require a higher amount of potash and phosphorus. Beans and tomatoes require less fertilizer, especially nitrogen, which can stimulate foliage growth at the expense of the fruit and pods. Both of these, however, do better with applications of phosphorus. Some

crops do better with relatively heavy fertilizer applications and include corn, onions, lettuce, spinach, celery, and the root crops.

Applying Fertilizer

Fertilizers are applied both at the time of planting and as a side-dressing. Fertilizers may be applied at the time of planting in one of three methods, and you may use all three or just one or two depending on the timing of application and the type of food-growing methods used.

The first application is broadcasting. After the ground has been tilled or worked up initially, broadcast the prescribed amount of fertilizer over

✪ Fertilizer can be applied in several ways. One of the most common is to broadcast the fertilizer over the growing site, using a push or hand-held broadcaster.

the soil surface. Use either a fertilizer spreader or broadcast by hand and then till the soil again to mix the fertilizer into the soil. If needed, limestone should be added at this time as well. This is the most costly in both time and expense but is commonly used in traditional row growing and when starting a new site, or at the first of the growing season before planting. You can also apply compost in this manner to begin a new garden or new season, and the method is called sheet composting. If growing in raised beds, this method is used, and you still have an economical and easy method of application, because you're using fertilizer only where the plants are located.

If you know the location of rows for crops, applying the fertilizer in the area of the rows also saves on time and expense. Mark off the row and dig a two- to three-inch deep furrow about three inches to each side of the marked row. Apply the fertilizer using the prescribed amounts. With most fertilizers, this will be about one to two pounds per one-hundred-foot of row. Cover the fertilizer with the soil, filling in the furrows. Then create a furrow for the seed in the row and plant the seed.

Plants that are set in hills (such as melons, squash, and cucumbers) and transplanted plants (such as cabbage, broccoli, lettuce and spinach grown in raised beds, as well as peppers and tomatoes) are often fertilized in the "hill" method. At the time of setting out the transplants, dig a hole about twice as deep as needed for the transplant roots. Add a couple of tablespoons of the prescribed fertilizer to the hole, cover with a couple of inches of dirt, water well, and set the transplants.

Liquid fertilizers are extremely easy to apply. I've been using Scotts Miracle-Gro for many years, and it can be applied with a sprinkler can or by combining with a soaker hose. Since it is both a foliage and root feeder, it can also be sprayed onto the plants with a sprayer available from the company. If growing your own plants from seed, use a fertilizer specifically mixed for seed growth. A number are available commercially, or you can make up your own. Fish emulsion or manures are both good choices. A starter fertilizer can also help your transplants get off to a good start. Again, these

can be purchased, or you can mix your own using a complete chemical or organic fertilizer. Add about two or three tablespoons of fertilizer to a gallon of water. Make sure the fertilizer is well dissolved. Stir before using and add about a cup of fertilizer around set plants. For tomatoes, peppers, and eggplants, use a solution of high phosphorus, such as 10-50-19. Slow-release fertilizers are available and are best for container gardening. More information on container gardening is in chapter 4, "Growing Foods in Small Spaces."

Liming

The proper pH is extremely important for productive food growing. Most vegetables grow best with a pH of 6.5 to 7.0, but most soils are acidic and require the pH to be raised. The most common method of raising the pH is to add limestone. Limestone works into the soil fairly slowly, at a rate of about one inch per year. Apply at least part of the limestone, as required by the soil test results, before tilling the soil. Use ground dolomite agricultural limestone. This comes in bag form and is easily applied. The material also adds calcium and magnesium, further improving the soil and making fertilizer elements more readily available. As a general rule, you should add two pounds per one hundred square feet of light soil and five and a half pounds per one hundred square feet of heavy soil. But follow the soil test suggestion.

❸ Fertilizing the rows or hills saves on fertilizer and avoids fertilizing any unwanted weeds.

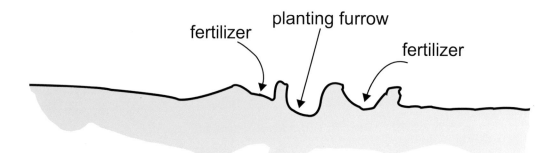

⊗ Liming is extremely important in many instances to raise the pH of acidic soil. In most instances ground dolomite agriculture limestone is used. Wood ash can also be used to raise the pH and also adds to soil fertility.

If you need a major change in pH, do so a step at a time—no more than one pH unit per year. Changes greater than one unit should be adjusted over a two- to three-year period. Again, your extension office can help you with this information.

Wood ash can also be used to raise the pH, and it has other elements that can help raise soil fertility. The following are the nutrients commonly found in wood ash:

Phosphorus–(1 to 2%)

Potassium, as potash–(5 to 25%)

Lime, as calcium carbonate–(30 to 50%)

Typically you need to use twice as much wood ash as you would with limestone. Unlike limestone, which is commonly applied in the fall, wood ash is best applied in the spring before planting, as the nutrients contained, especially the potash, leach easily from the soil. When collecting wood ash in the winter to spread in the spring, keep it in a dry place to prevent caking and losing nutrients.

Ground Preparation

You will need to break up the soil to grow anything, and the method used depends on the site, the size of the plot, and the type of equipment available or for rent, as well as the amount of work you wish to do. Very small plots and raised beds can be worked or created with nothing more than a spade or shovel. Make sure you remove all sod and work the soil deeply, turning it over so some of the subsoil mixes with the topsoil. Add humus and compost, fertilizing as you do.

The best food-growing gardens, however, are actually created in the late fall. Work at that time will pay off in less work throughout the growing season. Apply manure, fertilizer, humus in the form of compost, peat moss, or decomposed leaves, as well as limestone. Leave through the winter months, and then in the spring when the soil is dry enough to

❮ You will need to break up the soil in your planting site. A rotary tiller is the ideal tool and a good investment for larger gardens.

⊗ Smaller areas, such as raised beds, can be worked with a shovel.

crumble and will not ball up when a handful is squeezed, till, spade, or plow the materials under. An alternative is to grow a winter green fertilizer crop and then apply compost, well-dried cow manure, or other additives early in the spring as soon as the soil can be worked.

If you have a large site, and especially if it's a new garden area, you'll probably have to till it with a rotary tiller. On a large plot, you may need to hire someone with a tractor-powered tiller, although a walking tiller can be used if you have the time and energy. The old-time mold-board plow is still hard to beat for initial breaking up and turning over of the soil, but the site must then be graded and leveled with a harrow or cultivator. A rotary tiller is the best choice for most food growers. Not only can it be used for getting the site ready, but it can also be used to cultivate between rows during the season. Tillers do a better job than the traditional plows because they tend to mix the soil particles and organic matter.

If you're limited to the pick-and-shovel gang, the best tactic is a method called double-digging. Mark off the site with stakes and string.

Dig a trench about a foot wide and twelve to eighteen inches deep. Place the soil from this trench in a wheelbarrow or on a tarp. Dig another trench next to the first, placing the soil from this trench into the previously dug trench and turning the soil over if possible. Continue trenching until you get to the opposite side of the garden, then transport the soil from the first trench, and place it in the last trench.

You can work the soil in fall or spring. A fall tilling provides for earlier spring planting, but you won't be able to use a green manure or cover crop. Heavy soils, however, are best fall tilled to allow the freezing and thawing action of the winter to help break up the soil. Fall site work is also best if you're applying fairly large amounts of organic matter to build up the soil. With fall tilling or plowing, all you need to do in the spring is light tilling or harrowing. If spring tilling or plowing, wait for the right conditions. Plowing too early, while the soil is still wet and cold, can create cloddy clumps that will be a hassle the entire growing season. The ages-old test is to squeeze a handful of soil. If it crumbles easily, it's time to work the soil. If the soil squeezes into a ball or is sticky, it's too wet for good tillage. Plant as soon as you get the soil worked to get a head start on the weeds. In our garden, I time the spring tillage for specific plants. I till the areas for early plants and plant or set them, leaving the areas for later plants, such as corn, and tilling them immediately before planting.

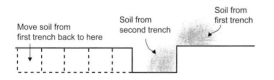

❨ Double digging is a good method for turning a sodded area into a growing site, or for creating a raised bed.

4

Growing Food in Small Spaces

Creating lush gardens in small spaces is nothing new. Replicating the Hanging Gardens of Babylon might be a bit impractical, but regardless of how tiny a space you have for growing your own food, you can use a variety of methods to grow a bountiful crop. Green zones can flourish on rooftops, patios, decks, and even pint-sized apartment balconies by using containers, raised beds, and also the Babylon-style vertical or even hanging gardening methods.

❮❮ You don't need a huge garden to grow your own food. Many foods can be grown in small spaces, using a variety of means.

Container Gardens

Container gardening offers many advantages. Containers can be used anywhere, but they're especially useful where space is a problem. You can place each container exactly where you want and rearrange them during the growing season for maximum effect. Pots and wooden boxes can be used to grow nearly anything, depending on the size of the containers; even dwarf fruit trees can be grown in containers.

Almost anything imaginable has been used at one time or another for container gardening, from discarded bathtubs to halves of wooden whiskey barrels. Large plastic buckets, with drainage holes cut in the bottom, can also serve as containers. Old recycled food coolers also make great, if somewhat ugly, containers.

» Containers for growing food can be any number of items including purchased pots.

Planter Boxes

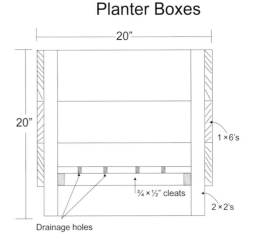

⌄ Even simple, do-it-yourself wooden boxes are effective for growing food.

« Container gardening is a great way of growing food on decks, patios, or even on an apartment balcony.

The most popular containers are clay or plastic pots and wooden boxes. The latter can be purchased or built at home if you're handy with your hands. Do-it-yourselfers have the advantage of building precisely to size and shape the boxes they need.

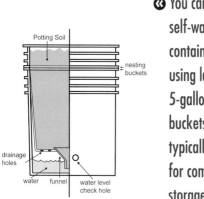

❮❮ You can build self-watering containers using large 5-gallon buckets typically used for commercial storage.

Box containers can be placed on a deck, patio, walkway or balcony, fastened to a window sill, or used as hanging planters on porches. Designs can be as simple or as elaborate as you like, and boxes can be crafted to suit your individual decorating or landscaping tastes. All containers must have drainage holes to prevent plants from drowning or rotting from too much water. You can even build your

❯❯ A soil mixture should be light and able to hold moisture and nutrients. Pebbles, gravel, or broken clay pot pieces can add to drainage.

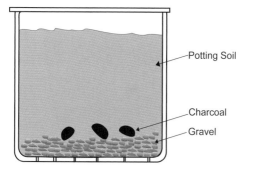

own "self-watering" containers. If you intend to place boxes or containers on a wooden surface such as a deck, it's a good idea to put shallow holding pans under them to catch excess water and prevent staining the deck. Another idea for large-sized containers on roofs, decks, and patios is to add wheels or make simple wooden dollies. This allows you to move the containers around for the best available light, or even indoors in the event of frost.

Regardless of design, wooden plant boxes need to be constructed of wood that is resistant to the ravages of weather, insects, and rot. Redwood and western cedar are two popular choices. Or use pressure-treated lumber for a long-lasting plant container. Whatever type of wood you use, make sure to also use exterior fasteners.

Another advantage of container gardening is that the soil used can be carefully prepared and matched to the specific needs of the plants you want to grow. As a general rule, the soil mixture should be fairly light and able to hold moisture and nutrients. It should also be able to drain well. The first step is to place a layer of pebbles, gravel, or pieces of broken clay pots in the bottom of the container to aid in

» Any number of foods can be grown in containers, including tomatoes in hanging baskets.

drainage. Some experts like to put a few pieces of charcoal in the bottom to help keep the soil "sweet." The boxes are then filled to within one-half inch or so of the top with soil. Use either purchased commercial potting soil mixes or make up your own using one part garden soil, one part compost or humus, and one part sand. Vermiculite or perlite can be substituted for sand to provide a lighter soil that will drain well, yet hold moisture. Another good recipe is six parts good, rich garden soil; one part peat moss; and two parts vermiculite or perlite. Some plants have specific alkaline or acid needs, and these can be met with soil additives. Your garden supplier or nursery should be able to help you with those. If you are gardening on a rooftop or balcony, consider using a growing medium without soil. It weighs about half as much as a soil mixture, which averages about twenty-five pounds per cubic foot. Planting mixtures without soil are available commercially, or you can make up your own. Use three parts peat moss and one part vermiculite or perlite. Add about a half pound of ground dolomitic limestone per each bushel to neutralize the acid in the peat moss.

All container-grown plants must be kept supplied with the proper nutrients according to the plants needs.

● Strawberries can be grown in the old fashioned strawberry jars, but can also be grown in a half-whiskey barrel planter with small holes cut around the sides.

holes

This is especially important for mixtures without soil. Liquid fertilizers such Miracle-Gro and other commercial products, as well as fish emulsion or homemade manure tea, should be applied once a week. Plants in containers also need to be kept well watered, and during summertime heat, that often means once or twice a day. Regularly check the soil. If the top inch is dry, water until the water begins to drain out. Container-grown plants must have at least six hours of light daily. If you don't have a place with full sun, consider making reflectors to help direct sun to the plants.

Any number of vegetables can be grown in containers, with tomatoes, peppers, herbs, onions, and lettuce some of the most popular. The small hot peppers are especially popular because they also add decor. A number of plant varieties are also available especially for growing in small spaces, such as dwarf cucumbers and so forth.

Strawberries are popular planted in the old-fashioned strawberry barrel, and these days "strawberry kits" complete with containers are available. Some plants, such as some varieties of tomatoes and cucumbers, can even be planted in hanging baskets.

Raised Beds for Supersmall Gardens

Raised beds also provide a lot of gardening in small spaces, regardless of whether you want to grow vegetables or herbs. In a way, raised beds are just big containers, and they have a number of advantages over traditional tilled-row gardening. Raised beds can be built and filled with an improved soil mixture in less time than it takes to develop a good in-ground plot. Raised beds also allow for intensive gardening, often called French intensive or square-foot gardening, raising more food in limited spaces. This means spacing plants much closer than in traditional gardening methods. Experts suggest it

⊗ One of the best ways of growing in small spaces, even in larger garden areas, is in raised beds.

takes five times as much space to grow food in conventional gardening.

With proper planting and care, you can produce over half a ton of vegetables in only a five-hundred-square-foot garden using these tactics. We have a number of raised beds in our garden. In fact, over half of our garden is made of raised beds, with mulched areas and walkways between. Built three feet wide, the beds allow you to reach to the center of the bed without walking on it or getting in it for planting, weeding,

and harvesting. Without the compaction of walking on the soil, the raised beds provide a continuously loose, friable soil. Older gardeners, such as me, find the heights of raised beds easier to work on since we can sit on the edge or on a stool and not have to stoop or bend as with ground-level plots. Raised beds take less time to plant and maintain as well. First, you don't need to till. Merely dig up the bed in early spring with a shovel or trowel, which is easy because the soil hasn't become compacted. An even

⊘ We grow a great deal of our food in raised beds. The beds are easier to work with, the soil stays soft and workable because it is not compacted, and we can grow a lot more food in a smaller space.

better method is to mulch the beds heavily in the fall.

Merely rake back the mulch in spring, uncover the loose soil, and plant. As the plants are growing close together, they also tend to shade out many of the weeds, cutting down on weeding. If raised with mulch, raised beds can almost eliminate weeding. And of course, harvesting and watering are also easier. With a little planning, you can direct water to specific beds or areas, cutting down on water and watering times.

Raised beds can also be combined with frames holding netting to keep out birds and other pests, as well as covered with plastic for winter gardening. One idea I've used is creating a "cage" of welded wire used for reinforcing concrete. This comes in five-foot-wide rolls, perfect for making cages for my 3 × 5 foot beds. It keeps out the deer, and adding mesh wire to the bottom keeps out the smaller critters such as rabbits. Covering the cage with clear plastic creates a mini-greenhouse for winter growing. There

⊗ Raised beds not only contain plants, but can also help keep out critters if covered with a wire mesh — which is great for those living in areas with an abundance of wildlife.

is one raised-bed intensive gardening problem you need to be aware of. If growing plants such as peppers in an intensive gardening method, they may cross-pollinate. Plant only one variety of each plant in each raised bed.

Raised beds are often combined with modern-day mulches such as black plastic or plastic screening mulch with microscopic holes that hold in moisture while holding down weeds for easy-care growing. This is a great way of growing strawberries that cuts down greatly on the weeding problem. Herbs do especially well in raised beds, and you can create an attractive herb garden by dividing the bed into sections for each variety of herbs.

Old-style raised-bed gardening consisted of mounding up the soil into long, raised, or rounded mounds with walkways between them. This is effective, but more intensive gardening can be done with contained beds. What makes a contained, raised bed is a border that holds the soil in place. My first beds were simply made of logs obtained by thinning the timber on our hillside farm. Concrete blocks, bricks, and rocks can all be

ⓧ Raised beds can be used with black plastic screening for weed-free growing of plants such as strawberries.

ⓧ You can create a formal and attractive herb bed using wood to create a divided raised bed.

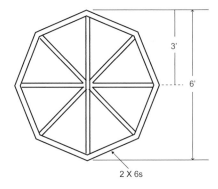

3'

6'

2 X 6s

ⓧ The easiest raised bed consists of simple raised mounds of soil with a walkway between the mounds.

used to build raised beds as can recycled railroad ties and landscaping timbers made of treated lumber specifically for use in creating raised-bed gardens.

These are often simply laid in place or held to sloping hillsides with wooden stakes. Cedar, redwood, or treated 2 × 6s or 2 × 8s can be fastened together with deck screws to create a fast, sturdy, and economical raised bed. They're basically boxes without bottoms.

Locate the bed where it will catch the most sun, full sun if possible, and then mark off the area with stakes and string. Use a shovel to dig out and

⊗ Containing the raised beds makes them easier to work with, increases their productivity, and keeps the soil in place.

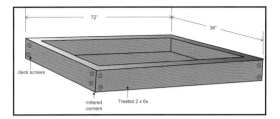

⊗ Raised beds can be contained many ways, including simple treated 2 x 6 frames. Ours are three feet wide and vary in length from 5 to 12 feet.

remove all sod, grass, and weeds. The best beds have very deep soil bases.

This is done by digging, if possible, down to at least eighteen to twenty-four inches. If you can't dig that deep, as in my area with rocks at about eight inches, simply build the beds higher.

Some of my beds are twelve inches high for that reason. Build the sides of the bed using the materials you've selected and reinforce the corners with stakes driven into the ground and fastened to the logs, timbers, or planks.

As with container gardening, soil that drains well and is rich in nutrients is the key to success. Both soil and nutrients should suit the plants you intend to grow. Because of the size and volume of a raised bed, you'll probably have to fill it with soil

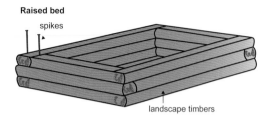

Raised bed

spikes

landscape timbers

❂ Landscape timbers can also be used to create a raised bed.

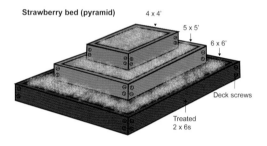

Strawberry bed (pyramid)

4 x 4'

5 x 5'

6 x 6'

Deck screws

Treated
2 x 6s

❂ One great way of growing strawberries is in a raised pyramid bed.

❂ You can grow plants more intensively in raised beds with closer spacing. Rather than planted in rows, plants are spaced in an equidistant triangular fashion. A cardboard template, sized to match the spacing, helps space plants properly. This chart shows the spacing.

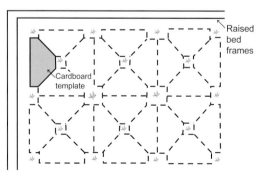

Raised bed frames

Cardboard template

materials readily available in your area or obtainable at a reasonable cost. As a general rule, a mixture of good topsoil, compost, or well-rotted manure, peat, and sand is a good starting point. Once the bed has been filled, have a soil sample tested to determine pH level and to see if any additional nutrients are required.

Intensive Growing Spacing Chart (equidistant in inches)	
Beans, Bush	6"
Beets	3"
Broccoli	15"
Cabbage	15"
Carrots	3"
Corn	12"
Cucumber	12"
Lettuce	6"
Melons	15"
Onions	5"
Peas	3"
Potatoes	10"
Radishes	1"
Spinach	3"
Squash	15"
Watermelon	12"

Another important factor in intensive gardening is to use precise and close plant spacing. Seeds or transplants are normally spaced equidistance apart. This will increase yields. One trick to getting more produce from intensive gardening is to set or seed plants in a staggered fashion rather than in rows. Make up a cardboard template in a triangle shape and use this to determine proper seed or transplant placement. This shape better utilizes the available space. But don't plant too closely. As a normal rule, you can about halve the spacing for plants such as lettuce, broccoli, and cabbage. We also simply sow lettuce and spinach on bare ground in a raised bed, rather than in individual rows, and shovel more loose compost and well-rotted manure over the seeds. The plants are then thinned as they sprout. We also interplant in raised beds, again adding to the intensive gardening tactic.

We often plant onions and lettuce together, lettuce or spinach, and cabbage or broccoli. The lettuce is harvested first, but as the broccoli gets bigger, it shades the lettuce, extending the lettuce harvest as well. And the lettuce cuts down on the weeds

⊗ Growing companion plants also helps save space. A tradition is planting beans, corn, and pumpkins next to one another.

until the broccoli gets started. Some food growers like to make a bed or two of the "big three"—corn, squash, and pole beans. The corn provides support for the pole beans, and the squash keeps down the weeds in the beans and corn. Another tactic we use is to keep the beds producing throughout the season with successive plantings—for instance, spring lettuce, followed by summer squash, followed by fall spinach. This is especially effective if you start seeds indoors, or in the summer on a porch or shady area, keeping plants ready to go into the beds at all times. Almost anything can be grown in raised beds in the intensive gardening method, even some plants you might not consider. You might even consider growing a fast-growing short or early corn in a raised bed. Space the seeds about six inches apart in all directions. Once the plants emerge, carefully weed and mulch heavily. Drive wooden stakes or steel posts in each corner of the bed and make a chicken wire cage around your mini corn patch. No pests, no fuss, and a bountiful supply of sweet corn from a very small space. A final trick to increasing yields is to keep produce regularly harvested. We pick tomatoes as soon as they begin to turn yellow or orange and allow them to ripen off the vine. They taste just as good as those left on the vine, and removing the tomatoes allows the plant to continue producing. The same tactic can be used with many other vegetables as well.

Vertical Gardening

Growing upward is a good choice when you don't have room to grow outward. We also use vertical gardening techniques in our garden as well. In fact, some plants—such as cucumbers, peas, pole beans, and even tomatoes—not only take up less space but also actually do better when grown vertically on supports. Fruits or vegetable are less likely to be damaged because they're not lying on the ground, and larger crops can be grown because their flowers are more exposed and therefore more likely to be pollinated. Grapes and berries, of course, all need to be supported by trellises or other means.

Fences are the simplest supports for some vertical gardening. For grapes or berries, fence posts should protrude six feet above ground level with no. 9 wire stapled to them. A fence for cucumbers and other plants that put out heavy vines can consist of sturdy hog wire stapled in place to the posts. My favorite support for growing cucumbers is a "cattle" panel.

This is a heavy-duty galvanized, welded-wire panel available at farm supply stores. Sixteen feet long and five feet high, it is supported by three steel posts and will grow lots of cukes well off the ground and easy to care for and pick.

Tomatoes are a very common and popular vertical-gardening plant. Tests have shown tomatoes will produce a great deal more grown

⊗ Keep vegetables picked to help the plant continue producing. We pick tomatoes as soon as they begin to turn orange.

⊗ Growing vertically can also help produce a lot of food in small spaces.

⊗ A cattle-panel, held in place with steel posts, makes a great permanent vertical support for cucumbers and other "climbers."

vertically rather than allowed to sprawl. The plants are traditionally tied to wooden stakes, but if you have a lot of plants, it can be a hassle keeping up with retying the fast-growing plants. The simplest method is to grow tomatoes in cages. These can be purchased, or you can make your own out of heavy wire. I made my first cages from hog wire, which creates a cage about four feet high. Then I discovered welded reinforcing wire normally used in concrete pours. This creates a five-foot cage that is much stronger and supports even the most prolific plants. As I discovered, the higher the cage, the more tomatoes are produced. My tomatoes will eventually grow right over the tops of the five-foot cages and hang down, still producing. Each of the two-and-a-half-foot diameter cages hold two plants, and with the right conditions and varieties, I've harvested almost fifty pounds of tomatoes from each cage. Our garden is on a hillside and can get pretty windy. Storms can blow the big cages over. I drive wooden stakes in beside the cages, spacing them about every third cage. I then tie the cages together and to the stakes. So far, this has prevented the cages from blowing over even in severe wind storms.

Pole beans also need support. These can be purchased supports, or you can make your own. A teepee of 2 × 2 poles or, in my case, saplings from the timber is a simple and easy method of constructing a pole bean support. Another type of support is an A-frame of 2 × 2s. This can be bolted together and then taken down at the end of the season if desired. Combine

✪ Tomato cages are an extremely productive way of growing tomatoes vertically and are, in fact, the best way of growing the fruit.

✪ Peas and cucumbers can also be grown on garden panels made of 1 x 4s covered with chicken wire and supported by posts.

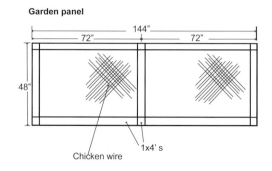

Garden panel

Portable pyramid bean tower

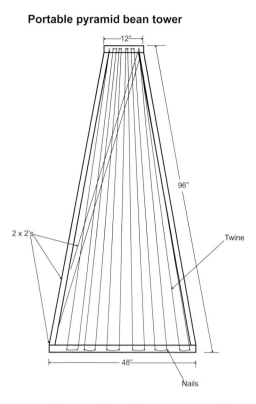

⊗ A simple, portable pole bean tower can be made from 2 x 2s and twine.

⊗ An A-frame support can also be made from 2 x 2s and set over a raised bed for intensively raising pole beans.

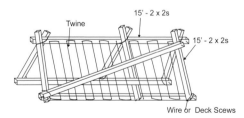

the A-frame support with a raised bed and you can raise a lot of beans in a very small space.

Regardless of how tight your gardening space is, a little ingenuity and the right methods can help make your world a little more green. More elaborate systems can be created if you're interested in decor as well as growing food. Don't let the thought of a big garden deter you from growing your own food. These gardening methods can be combined to grow a lot of food in a small space.

⊗ You can even grow cucumbers and other plants vertically in containers with a simple box container and a trellis-like support.

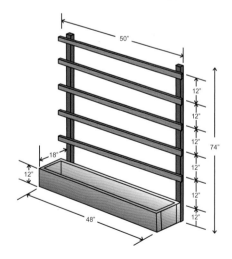

5

Growing Vegetables

Selecting Seeds and Plants

Most vegetables are available in a confusingly wide number of varieties. Some varieties take longer to mature; some produce smaller or larger fruits. With vegetables like tomatoes and corn, there can also be a wide variance in flavors. It's important when choosing seeds or plants for growing your own food to match the variety to your garden site, geography, and locale. Seed companies offer an array of both seeds and plants. Most seed catalogs,

❮❮ Vegetables are available in an amazing number of varieties. There are, in fact, whole catalogs just of tomato varieties, including this yellow pear tomato.

⊗ It's important to match the plant species and variety to your growing site, topography, and weather.

however, describe which varieties are best for certain specific parts of the country or certain zones. You will also, of course, want to select varieties with a flavor you like.

The first-time food grower will need to do a lot of experimenting to find the best choices. Talking with other local growers can be a great help. If purchasing vegetables from a local farmer's market, ask about the variety. Eventually you'll discover favorites that not only suit your tastes but are also easier to grow in your particular garden. Trying new varieties

of vegetables, however, is half the fun of growing your own food.

Some vegetables are available only as seeds while others as seeds or plants. If you're just getting started, your local garden center can usually help in selecting seeds or plants that are good producers in your area. Farm supply stores are also an excellent source of local seeds. Some seeds—for instance, corn—are more economical purchased in bulk from these local sources than by mail order. Other seeds that are cheaper in bulk include the standard lettuce varieties,

⊗ Some plants are available as seed and others as plants, ready to transplant.

an almost endless supply of chain super-store, as well as mail-order plants are available. Vegetable and flower plants must be a very high mark-up items because there seems to be a growing number of market-ers. I've noticed over the years the cost of these plants has also become increasingly high. The most popular and traditional plants are tomatoes, peppers, cabbage, broccoli, and cau-liflower, but any number of vegetables are available these days.

beets, spinach, and turnips. Potato sets, onion sets, and plants are also more economical purchased locally and are usually suited to the area. On the other hand, you are more limited in the availability of many plant vari-eties, for instance, tomatoes, peppers, and corn, even lettuce. Mail order may be your only source for some seed varieties.

Many vegetables, such as corn, are best direct seeded into the gar-den. Other vegetables can be either direct seeded or started indoors or in a greenhouse and then transplanted into the garden. Many of the latter are available as plants in flats or pots, ready to set out in your garden. Today

Sowing Seeds Indoors

Starting your own seeds indoors and then transplanting into your garden is easy, fun, and a great way of saving on

⊗ You can easily start many seeds indoors for transplanting outdoors.

growing your own food. In addition, you can grow plant varieties not available locally. Growing your own food is a continual learning process, and the past few years I've started seeds indoors for an increasingly wider variety of plants. This has allowed us to greatly extend our growing season. In addition to tomatoes, peppers, broccoli, cabbage, and cauliflower, plants started from seed now include beets, lettuce, spinach, and even onions. Some vegetables, however, are harder to transplant into the garden and are best direct-seeded. The volume of some plants needed also makes direct seeding the best choice.

Seeds can be started and grown just about anywhere in your house. I've started seeds indoors for many years, even in my basement, using a fluorescent tube for light. A small greenhouse or sunny window can, however, be a helpmate. We have a very small lean-to greenhouse that is passively solar heated used to start several hundred transplants in each season. We start some seeds indoors and move them out to the greenhouse to continue growing until it is time to set them out. Later, plants are started directly in the greenhouse.

The most important factor in growing your own seeds indoors is when to sow the seeds to set out the transplants at the right growing stage and in the right weather conditions. If you start seeds indoors too early, they'll be spindly and hard to transplant by the time you finally can get them set out. Too late and they may be too tender to withstand transplanting. To start seeds indoors, you'll need to know three things: the last expected frost date for spring gardens and the first expected frost date for fall gardens, the type of weather the young plant grows best in, and the number of weeks from sowing to setting out size of the plants. Although nationwide frost charts are available, these

⊗ It's important to start seeds at the correct time so you can transplant them at the appropriate time of the season. Many seed packets provide this crucial information.

are pretty general. Whether you live at low or high elevation in your local area, you can also have a great deal of influence on the frost dates for your garden. Your local county extension office can provide much more detailed information for your growing area. In addition to frost dates, other seasonal benchmarks are also important. Some vegetables germinate at different temperatures. For instance, some seeds need temperatures of 70°F or warmer, while others germinate best at 55°F or cooler. Some young vegetable plants grow best in cool weather while others thrive in warm and hot weather. The temperatures referred to are soil, not air, temperatures.

As you can guess, all seeds are not started at the same time. For instance, we start broccoli and cabbage on January 1; tomatoes and peppers are

◉ You can purchase or make up a seed starting kit. Shown is a simple wooden-flat suspended over a heat mat and is self watering.

not started until mid-March. It helps to make up a planning chart or calendar for the different vegetables you plan to grow. The chart should list the following: seed type, transplant season, transplant date in your area, number of weeks from sowing to garden size transplants, and date to sow. To decide when to sow, pick the right date for setting out in your garden and then count back the number of weeks needed to grow the plants to the right size for setting out. Seed packets have this information: for instance, tomato seed packets suggest seeding six weeks before setting out. In our area, the last frost is late April, and we plan to set out on May 1, so tomato seeds are started mid-March as stated before. Once you've decided when to start your seeds, sort the seed packages according to the best starting dates for each.

In addition to the seeds, you'll also need some supplies. First is a seed-starting medium. A number of these are available commercially, or you can make up your own. The medium should be porous, well drained yet absorbent, and loose and friable, not heavy. Finely textured humus or compost is often used. One of the most

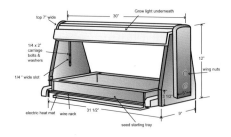

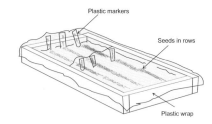

⊗ Seeds can be started and grown near a sunny window, but a grow-light suspended over the plants provides more consistent results.

⊗ Seeds are started in rows in tiny furrows. Plastic seed markers cut from plastic food dishes and a piece of plastic food wrap create a mini-greenhouse.

common home mixes is a blend of peat moss and perlite or vermiculate, as well as one part finely sifted compost to five parts of the peat moss-perlite mix. This adds some fertilizer. In addition, you'll need seed-starting trays. These can be purchased as seed-starter kits, some even with starting medium and a clear plastic cover. You can also make up your own quite economically using a number of recycled items.

Any number of tactics can be used, depending on the number of plants you intend to grow and your growing area. I've created a very easy, consistently successful seed-starting technique. The technique utilizes warm heat and bottom watering, along with a grow light above.

These units are sold through many seed catalogs and are very efficient,

⊗ When the plants have three leaves they're ready to transplant into pots or individual plant trays.

⊗ The seedlings can be transplanted into any number of containers, from purchased pots and trays to recycled foam plastic cups. One of my favorites is rolled newspaper pots.

❄ Double a piece of newspaper and cut it to fit the size of a vegetable can, with about an inch extra. Roll the paper around the can.

but I've constructed my own quite economically. A solid plastic tray has two holes bored in it. Sections of soft rope are threaded through the holes, and the rope is laid out on the bottom of the plastic tray. The rope extends out to the bottom of the tray, and the ends are placed in a plastic pan of water. The water gently wicks up the rope into the seed-starting tray.

The seed-starting tray sits on a wire rack over the top of an electric heat pad made just for starting seeds. Over the top of this is a rack holding a fluorescent grow light. A piece of kitchen plastic wrap over the soil keeps in moisture and provides a warmer temperature until the tiny seeds first sprout; then the plastic is removed.

This is where I depart from many other tactics. All my early-season seeds are thickly sown in rows. The growing medium is placed in the tray and well watered until it is thoroughly soaked. Or you can place the growing medium in a plastic bag and add water until it is well soaked and then add to the starting tray. In either case, the starting medium must be well flattened and pressed out smooth. I use a piece of one-quarter-inch thick plywood (or recycled paneling) to press tiny "furrows" or indentations in rows in the tray. Seeds are dropped into the furrows and covered lightly with more starting medium, the amount of covering depending on seed depth requirements. Normally seeds are covered to about twice their thickness and the starting medium pressed down to assure soil contact. Some seeds will not germinate without light and should not be covered. Check the instructions on the seed packet. I cut plastic food containers such as cottage cheese containers into one-half-inch-wide strips and about one and a half inches long. I mark the different varieties with these "row markers." Plastic wrap is placed over the tray and over the tops of the row markers; the top light and bottom heat pad are both turned on. The unit is left to run twenty-four hours a day until the seedlings emerge, and then the plastic is removed. It's important to check twice a day and fill the water container as needed. In a few days or a week, seedlings will sprout, and the plastic wrap is removed. Using this method, I start several hundred seedlings in a very small space.

When the seedlings become large enough to have two actual leaves, they are transplanted into individual pots to continue growing until they are ready to be set out. I've recycled any number of items into pots to hold the individual plants. This includes reusing plastic trays from purchased plants, foam plastic drink cups, and my favorite rolled-up newspaper pots.

These not only recycle newspapers but can also be used with plants that don't transplant well because they are set out in the pots without disturbing the roots. Foam plastic cups must have a hole punched in their bottoms for water drainage. Paper pots do tend to dry out faster than plastic ones, so make sure to keep them well watered.

Place the individual pots or plant containers into a solid plastic tray. Fill each with a good potting soil mix and you're ready to transplant. The potting soil can be purchased or homemade. A simple recipe is one bushel of peat, one bushel of perlite or vermiculite, one bushel of compost, and one-half cup ground limestone. Add nutrients if you wish, even matching each plant's special needs, but keep the amounts fairly low.

Water the pots and then use a wooden pencil to poke a hole in the center of the planting medium. Using a wooden popsicle stick, dig under and gently pry up a few seedlings. Gently separate the plants by holding them by their leaves. Place the roots down in the hole in the medium and use the eraser end of the pencil to press the soil around the roots.

Mark each tray or pot as to variety. I use the plastic strips for trays and

⊗ Tape the end of the paper in place.

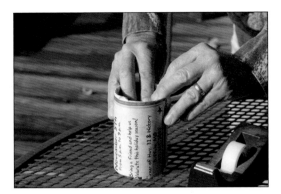

⊗ Push the extra length of paper down inside the cup.

⊗ Remove the cup and insert it bottom-side down into the paper tube to compress the bottom folded section tightly together.

write on foam cups with a felt marker. Water well and place in a slightly cooler, but not cold, but sunny place for the seedlings to continue to grow properly. Keep well watered by bottom watering. The soil shouldn't dry out but shouldn't drown the plants either.

Seeds for lettuce, spinach, melons, and others are started in individual pots. I sow seeds that don't mind having their roots disturbed—like lettuce, spinach, and beets—in the wooden trays. In this case, the plants are divided by cutting around each plant with a dull knife and separating the roots at transplanting time. This only works with plants that don't mind having their roots disturbed.

Presprouting is a good tactic for seeds that are hard to sprout or expensive and scarce. Dampen a double layer of paper towels and place the seeds on the towel, making sure they do not touch. Roll the towel up, making sure the seeds don't shift. Label a plastic bag with the seed name and place the roll into the plastic bag.

⊗ Regardless of the containers used, fill with a good potting soil, water well, and use a fat pencil to poke a hole in the soil in the center of the containers.

⊗ Use a Popsicle stick or similar item to gently pry a seedling from the starting tray.

⊗ Place the seedling roots-down in the hole, as deeply as possible without covering the leaves. Use the eraser end of the pencil to gently press in place. Then press soil around the seedling.

Partially close the bag. The seeds should have some air. Place in a warm spot. In two days check the seeds to see if they have sprouted and then check daily until the seeds sprout. Once they sprout, place in individual containers. Be sure not to damage the tender roots and stems.

The more traditional method of starting seeds indoors is to start them in individual pots or plant trays. In this case, the trays or pots are placed in a large plastic tray, and the starting medium is added and moistened. Two seeds are placed in each "cell" or pot. The trays or pots are covered with plastic wrap and the holding tray placed in a warm area with at least 70°F temperature. The top of a refrigerator or hot-water heater is a traditional choice, or you may use any gentle heat source. You won't need light for the seeds to germinate.

Begin checking after the first couple of days and then check daily for the first sprouts. Once the seeds sprout, remove the plastic and place the tray in a slightly cooler spot, around 60° to 65°F, but with plenty of sunlight. Near a patio door or a large window is a good choice. Turn the tray each day to prevent the seedlings from growing sideways toward the light. If the seedlings miss a day of light, they will become spindly. Again, the best tactic is to use a bank of fluorescent tubes. Keep the bulbs two to three inches away from the seedlings and allow at least sixteen hours of light a day. Water two or three times a day to keep the

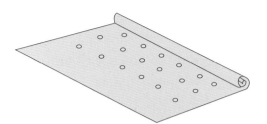

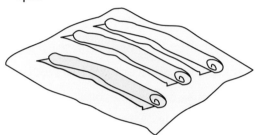

⊗ Some seeds do best presprouted. Place in dampened paper towels and then insert the towels into a plastic bag and place in a warm spot.

⊗ The more traditional method of starting seeds is in individual cells of plastic trays. Plant two seeds to each cell and snip off one when the seedlings have emerged.

soil from drying out, but water lightly to prevent disturbing the soil. This is especially important if the plants are near a window. Don't overwater and drown the plants or keep them so wet a fungus forms. Bottom watering is the best tactic. Keep a close eye on your seedlings. If they bend over and wilt, the soil is too dry. If they bend over with a break at soil line, the soil is too wet, creating a damping-off that can kill your entire crop of seedlings. Damping-off is also sometimes caused by poor air circulation. Allow the surface of the soil to dry out slightly, but do not let the bottom dry.

Once the plants set two pairs of leaves, use a pair of sharp scissors to snip off one of the plants, leaving only one plant per cell or pot. Once a week, feed the seedlings with a diluted liquid fertilizer, such as fish or seaweed emulsion, compost tea, or a commercial liquid fertilizer. If growing under lights, continue to move the lights up so they stay just a few inches above the tops of the plants. Placing a small fan near the seedlings will help keep the plants dry and fungus free, as well as keep the air stirred around them, creating a better supply of carbon dioxide. Provide more water, but less frequently, and feed with the diluted fertilizer. At this time, about April 1 in my area, all my growing transplants

⊘ Place seedlings in a sunny location. We use our small greenhouse.

are moved into my small greenhouse for further growth. It's crowded, but it works. At about five weeks, you may wish to repot the plants into larger three- or four-inch pots or trays. This will provide sturdier-, larger-stemmed plants for transplanting.

Use a flat wooden stick to gently lift out the plant and place in the larger pot half filled with potting soil. Press soil around the plant and water. Make sure the transplant is planted deep, up to the lower leaves. Growing into garden-size plants may take just a few more days, or a week or so, depending on the variety. It's best to be able to transplant into the garden before the plants begin flowering.

Hardening Off

Hardening off is a very important step in successfully transplanting your carefully grown seedlings. The young plants have been coddled and well taken care of. If you set them out in the garden immediately, they'll suffer from sun, wind, and rain. Harden the tender young plants by moving your transplant trays outdoors to a shady spot out of the wind. Start with an hour a day, increasing the time each day and bringing the trays back in at nighttime. Keep the plants well watered, but they will wilt somewhat even at that, so don't get too worried. The plants will perk back up when brought inside. After a couple of days in the shade, move them into a partially sunny location for a couple of more days. Then move to a sunny spot for a day or two, and the plants are hardened and ready to transplant.

Transplanting

Proper transplanting is also important. Transplant late in the afternoon if possible so the plants don't start their first day with full sun. Make sure your garden or bed is well prepared to receive the transplants. Position the plants, still in the pots where you want them, to achieve proper spacing. Dig holes with a shovel or trowel for each

⊗ Properly transplanting seedlings is important. Transplant in late evening. Dig a hole and set the plant gently in place.

⊗ Press the soil firmly around the roots and water well.

plant. A bulb planter works well for small plants. Add water to each hole. Setting the plants to the correct depth and in the correct position is important. Some plants, such as cabbage and lettuce with base branches, should not have their stems buried. Other plants, such as peppers and tomatoes, do better if buried deeper. But never bury the leaves. If you bury part of the stem,

pinch off the leaves. Keep debris such as sticks or leaves out of the transplanting hole.

Press the soil firmly down around the transplants and water well. It's important to thoroughly soak the soil with water to "water-in" the transplants. In beds, the soil should be wet to several inches below the surface. One tactic is to soak the beds just before planting. Widely spaced plants should be watered until a water puddle forms around the base of the plants. This helps to eliminate air pockets and creates better soil and root contact. Adding a mulch as soon as the plants are set out and watered can help the transplants get off to a good start and will prevent weeds from competing with the young plants. Use old or weathered mulch, not fresh organic materials. Old hay, straw, dry grass clippings, and wood shavings are good choices. Make sure the mulch is up around the plants, but be careful not to break the stems.

Direct Seeding

Many vegetables are direct seeded into the garden. This can be done in several ways, depending on the plants,

⊗ Many plants, such as beans and corn, are planted in rows.

Marking Rows

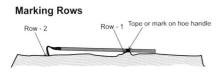

⊗ A marker on a hoe or rake handle can be used to help evenly space rows.

timing, and so forth. Make sure your garden is well prepared and the timing is correct for the seed chosen. Direct seeding in the soft soil of raised beds is easy. Simply push the seeds into the soil with your finger to the depth and at the spacing needed. Water and wait for the seedlings to emerge. For row seeding, first mark out the rows. The distance between rows depends on the vegetable variety, as well as the gardening method and tools. If you plan to till between the rows, leave room for your tiller.

If you plan to hoe or mulch between the rows, plant somewhat closer but still stick fairly close to the suggested row spacing for each variety. I keep a piece of black plastic electricians' tape around a hoe handle. The distance from the head of the hoe to the tape is the correct width between rows for my tiller. Some plants need wider spacing, for instance, beans need more than corn because of their bushy growing habit.

Most plants are grown in rows. To make rows, tie a piece of heavy string to a couple of stakes, drive the stakes in place at either end of the proposed row, and use the corner or edge of a hoe to dig a furrow with the correct depth for the seeds. Drop the seeds at the correct spacing. You may prefer to seed thicker than the final spacing and thin plants to assure a completely full row. For instance, I plant corn in this manner, making sure the entire row is thickly planted and thin after the plants are up. Add fertilizer before or after planting, depending on the variety or species. Remove the string line and use a garden rake to bring the soil back over the furrow and cover the seeds. I like to use the back of the rake to gently compress or pack the soil down on the seeds to assure good soil contact. Some plants, such as the tiny seeds of lettuce, need light to germinate. Just cover lightly. All that's left is to water and wait.

Watering

Successfully growing food requires water. Some method of regularly supplying water to your plants, whether transplants or direct seeded, is required. In some parts of the country, watering plants may be a problem. Droughts and restricted water use may require the use of collected rainwater in some areas. Any number of ways can be used to conserve water, yet supply moisture to your plants. One of the most important steps begins at seeding time. Keep the seedbed

⊗ A much better method that utilizes less water and places water only where it is needed is a soaker hose. Used with mulch, it's extremely effective.

moist until the seeds have sprouted. Do not allow it to dry out. Use a fine spray with your hose nozzle or watering can to prevent washing soil away from the rows or from around transplants. Rain is, of course, your best source of water. Once seeded or planted, your garden will need about one inch of rain per week, depending on evaporation. You'll need slightly more in the summer months. If this is lacking or you notice plants wilting during the heat of the day, they're not getting enough water. Check the soil moisture weekly, especially during the first three weeks of planting. If the top couple of inches of soil are dry, you'll need to water. Later in the season, as the roots grow deeper, you'll need to

⊗ In most areas and instances you'll have to supply water to your garden. This can be done in numerous ways. A sprinkler is one of the most common.

water less. It's best to water deeply and less frequently than lightly and more frequently. Soak thoroughly at each watering. In summer, this may mean watering for up to four hours or more. Allow the upper portion of the soil to dry out slightly before watering again. This helps to increase root growth.

Water can be provided for plants in a number of ways. Soaker hoses are one of my favorite methods of watering rows. Soaker hoses, as well as trickle tubes, allow for deep soaking of the soil and don't apply water to foliage, which can cause disease problems. I've recycled a number of broken old soaker hoses by cutting them to fit exactly the space needed and then putting new hose ends on them. It's easy and efficient to use these hoses under mulch, providing the best and simplest moisture management system. I even use soaker hoses on my corn patch, which often consists of five or six rows at least fifty feet long. I lay the soaker hose next to one row, water for a couple of hours, turn off the hose, pull it out, and pull it back into the next row, continuing until the entire corn patch is well watered. You can also position a liquid fertilizer feeder just before the hose.

A number of mechanical watering devices are available. Impulse sprinklers can provide a lot of water to a large area but tend to beat down small or tender plants. An oscillating or whirling sprayer provides a finer mist, and many can be adjusted to water only a specific area. The simplest method, however, is the old-fashioned garden watering can. Raised beds and small gardens are easily watered with these. It's easy to add fertilizer to the watering can and water and feed your plants at the same time.

A simple method I've used with hilled plants, such as melons and cucumbers, is to punch holes in plastic food containers and place them

⊗ Hilled plants can be grown easily using black plastic or other mulch and a plastic container with holes punched in the bottom. Fill with water or add water soluble fertilizer or manure tea.

in holes next to the plants. Fill with water and allow the water to seep through the bottom and to the plant roots. Again, you can easily add liquid fertilizer or manure tea to feed the plants at the same time.

Thinning and Weeding

Once your seedlings are up, it's important to thin them to the spacing instructions on the seed packet or to the information in chapter 6 on "Vegetable Specifics." It's also extremely important to keep your garden weeded. Weeds provide direct competition for food, and if they get too high, weeds can also shade out the sun. Hand weeding and hoeing were much hated chores by many country kids who were required to help. I know! I was one of the kids that never wanted to raise a garden when I grew up.

Mulch

Mulching can be one of the most important tools for growing your own food. Not only does it conserve water, but it also keeps the soil from hard panning and provides a lighter

⊗ Mulching makes growing your own food much easier.

⊗ Any number of materials, including sawdust or wood chips, may be used as mulch.

soil for roots to more easily grow. And it keeps down weeds. You really can't mulch too much, unless you cover the leaves of your plants. Just about any plant can be mulched although it takes time, effort, and a fairly large amount of materials to mulch a big corn patch. The best thing about mulching is once done, you've cut your gardening chores greatly for the rest of the season. Mulch should be applied as soon as plants are up and thinned. Any number of materials can be used as mulch. Regardless of what is used, the mulch should be dried, not green.

Common mulching materials include the following: straw, old hay, leaves, dried grass clippings, sawdust, and wood chips. Some folks have had good luck using old newspapers for mulch. We feed calves at weaning time from our cow-calf operation and end up with a supply of paper feed sacks. They recycle great

Material	Advantages	Disadvantages	Use
Tree bark, wood chips	Slow to decompose	Large chunks	Decorative
Tree trimmings	Inexpensive, readily available	Needs to be composted or shredded. Can introduce disease	Decorative
Pine needles	Slow to decompose	Acidic	For acid-loving plants
Sawdust	Good soil builder and weed preventer	Acidic, can deplete nitrogen	Around all plants
Straw	Excellent weed preventer, readily available	Lasts only one season	All plants
Grass clippings	Excellent weed preventer, readily available	Lasts only one season, could contain herbicides	All plants
Leaves	Readily available, lightweight	Acidic, can blow away	Toxic to brassicas

❂ Any number of natural items can be used for mulch.

into mulching materials around my tomato plants and under the tomato cages. It's important to provide plenty of mulch, usually four to six inches is a minimum, and you'll probably need to add more mulch as the season progresses.

Black plastic can also be used as mulch, and it's a great way of warming up the soil in northern areas for quicker garden starts or extending the growing season in the fall. I use black plastic to provide a total mulch for melons. The plastic covers the entire patch with holes cut for each melon "hill." The melons sprawl over the black plastic as they grow, and there are no weeds between and around the vines.

⊗ Black plastic is an effective mulch for many plants, including melons and cantaloupes.

Feeding

You'll also need to side-dress or apply fertilizer of some sort as the season progresses. Yellowish leaves and a slow growth usually indicate a lack of nutrients. The type of fertilizer, amount applied, and method depends on the plant and your garden soil nutrients. Chapter 6 on "Vegetable Specifics" details fertilizing for different varieties. Most plants need a bit of nitrogen side-dressing. The amount and timing are important.

⊗ Most plants need to be side-dressed with some sort of fertilizer during the season.

Diseases and Pests

A healthy garden, with good garden soil and cared for properly, will have fewer pests and diseases than an ill-kept garden. Many diseases are caused by poor gardening tactics. Several simple practices can help prevent diseases and insect infestations. Overwatering or watering at the wrong time and keeping foliage wet can be a major cause of several diseases. Water in early afternoon to allow foliage to dry before nightfall. If you have long periods of wet weather, you may wish to consider using a fungicide on some plants. One easy step is to choose disease-free plants and seeds. This is especially important if you have diseases specific to your area. Seed companies list plants and seeds that are immune to specific diseases.

In addition to diseases, a whole host of creatures love the food you grow, or at times seemingly attempt to grow. One of the best preventive methods is to rotate your plants. Don't grow the same plant year after year in the same spot to prevent the spread of soil-borne diseases. This is especially important for plants such as potatoes and tomatoes. Keep your garden clean. Remove all debris at the end of

❷ Disease and bugs can be a problem. They can be combated in a number of ways. Keeping a clean garden—free of debris—is necessary. Some bugs can also be handpicked for control.

the season. Fall tilling and then planting a green cover crop will also expose and kill some of the insects and insect eggs that overwinter in garden debris. Keeping a continuous watch on your plants is important to stop infestations before they become major problems. Watch for signs of insect problems, including chewed leaves, droppings, and the insects themselves. Handpick occasional pests, but be ready to apply insecticides before pests begin multiplying. Again, proper garden hygiene can go a long way in cutting back on insect populations.

If you spot heavy infestations, it's time to do battle. A number of ways are available to battle infestations, but how you combat this army is your choice. I tend to use a combination of methods. When my kids were little, I paid them as insect bounty hunters. A hornworm off the tomato patch meant a dime in their piggy bank. Colorado potato beetles went for a penny apiece, as did squash bugs. Slugs were also a dime apiece. Companion planting can combat some pests. For instance, interplanting marigolds along with vegetables such as cabbage and broccoli can cut down on pests. A number of natural remedies are available for helping to control insect pests, as are chemical pesticides. Keep your garden well weeded. Weeds can harbor insect pests and diseases.

Chemical pesticides or insecticides are extremely effective in controlling insect infestations, but in some cases, they also destroy beneficial insects, even some that prey on harmful insects. If you decide to use chemical pesticides, make sure you carefully follow all label directions. Measure accurately. Don't spray when there is any wind. Follow all safety precautions in mixing and handling and wear protective clothing. Always follow the specific days-before-harvest information for that particular chemical. In most instances, this means two weeks before harvest. Many pests and diseases are specific to regional areas. Check with your local county extension office for further information on controlling diseases and pests in your area.

Critter Control

If the insect army isn't enough, there are also more and bigger critters ready to feed off your efforts. Living in the Missouri Ozark hills means living with

❯ Wild critters from rabbits to deer can also be a major problem when growing your own food.

wildlife, and there's a lot of it around our home, including deer, turkeys, rabbits, squirrels, ducks, and geese, as well as lots of snakes, field mice, moles, groundhogs, possums, raccoons, and gophers, not to mention thousands of songbirds such as blue jays that love fruits. We thoroughly enjoy the wildlife, but when it comes to growing our food, it's a different matter. When I was younger and had more energy, I simply planted enough for all. But these days I'm more protective of my food garden. I plant lots of food plots scattered around our property just for the wildlife, but that won't keep critters out of the garden.

We've tried just about everything to keep the critters under control. Raccoons in the corn patch have been the worst. A neighbor suggested I run an extension cord to my patch and hang a floodlight. I did and they hit the patch again that night. Then he suggested I add a radio. I did and they hit the patch again. All we did was provide music and lights for their party. My young son Michael had a big old Lab called Fireball that went everywhere with

❮ Simple cages can be constructed around raised beds to keep out the critters. Cage shown is from concrete reinforcing wire.

Michael. I hit on the idea of parking my pickup next to the corn patch, putting a sleeping bag in the back of the truck for Michael. We thought Fireball would stay close to Michael and keep the coons out of the corn. The next morning when I looked at the patch, it had been devastated again. Michael was in his sleeping bag asleep, but so was Fireball.

A good fence can go a long way toward protecting a small garden. It must, however, be deer high, rabbit short, and groundhog tough to be effective. The fence can be constructed of many things, but one extremely effective permanent fence is made from sections of cattle panels fastened to steel posts driven into the ground. This creates a sturdy five-foot-high fence. To keep the smaller critters out, include a section of poultry wire around the bottom.

If you don't want to enclose the whole garden, an alternative is to use wire cages over raised beds or row covers. Wire cages made of welded concrete reinforcing wire are effective for deer, and you can also add poultry wire for smaller critters. One advantage these have is you can simply place plastic over the cages

⊗ One of the best methods of critter control is an electric fence.

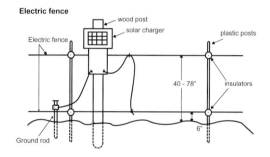

⊗ Designed properly, an electric fence will keep out small and large critters.

to create miniature greenhouses for early spring or late fall and winter food growing.

Fencing

An electric fence is the only cure we've found for marauding coons and deer. We use one low strand for keeping out raccoons and groundhogs and one high strand for deer. My neighbors have the ultimate in an electric fence,

⊗ You can save seeds from some plants to grow your own. Only seeds from heirloom, standard, and non-hybrid plants can be saved. Place seeds in paper towels in a safe place to dry, then store in envelopes.

and they need it for the large deer population in the area. Their fence consists of closely spaced electric wires spaced from just a few inches off the ground to the top strand at almost five feet off the ground. An electric fence consists of a charger, which can be plugged into a household circuit, or solar powered.

No, the electric fence won't electrocute animals. A good, powerful charger, however, will give them a hefty charge, and it doesn't take animals long to learn to avoid it. You will also need posts and wire. A portable fence can be set up with plastic push-in posts and a wire called polywire, which consists of plastic wire interlaced with fine metal wires. Tape wire is also available, and it's more visible and carries more current. Both are economical, easy to install and take down, and use. For a permanent fence, use metal posts, insulator connectors on the posts, and wire or tape fencing.

6

Vegetable Specifics

Each type of vegetable has different growing requirements. The amounts of seed, the number of plants needed per person, when and where to plant—these are all important for the serious food grower. Below are the details of how to grow each specific vegetable.

***

Beans (bush, pole, filet, lima, and shell or dry beans)

Description. In their many different types, beans are one of mankind's most important foods. And they're

❮ Beans, such as green snap beans, are some of the most important and easiest of foods to grow.

⊗ Bean varieties include both bush and pole types.

easy to grow. If you were to grow only one vegetable, beans would be a good choice. They're great fresh, canned, dried, or frozen. Beans belong to the legume family with other foods, such as snap peas, soybeans, lentils, and peanuts. Beans are a very important source of fiber, as well as high in protein. Beans are also virtually fat and cholesterol free and are full of vitamins.

Types. Beans are available in both bush and pole varieties. Bush beans tend to put on a main crop, followed by successive crops, and are good fresh and for canning or freezing. Bush beans grow as bushes or close to the ground. They do not need supports, but some varieties tend to produce more sprawling plants, taking up more space and allowing beans on the bottom to contact the ground. Pole beans mature over a longer season, but with less initial productivity. This makes them good choices for picking and eating a continuous crop of fresh beans. Pole beans require seven- to eight-foot poles or supports for their vines. Since pole beans are up off the ground, they are usually cleaner because of less splattering with soil in heavy rains and are easier to pick. Snap and lima beans are available as both bush and pole. Bush beans can be sown every two weeks to provide a continuous supply throughout the summer.

The following are the kinds of beans you may consider growing:

Snap beans. By far the most popular type of bush snap beans include

❰ Bean varieties also include limas as well as types that are often dried such as navy and pinto beans.

the wide variety of green beans. These include many of the classic home garden plants. Another type is the yellow wax bean, producing the bright yellow snap beans often used in the popular three-bean salad. These beans tend to mature more slowly. Italian or Roma beans are a flatter version with a more pronounced and rich bean flavor. Filet beans are a traditional and favorite European bean, often used as baby French green beans. They have some of the tendencies of both bush and pole with long string-free pods. Pole snap beans include a number of green beans, as well as wax and Romano.

Lima beans. Limas love hot climates. They are available as the smaller-seeded bush as well as pole beans. The bush lima beans tend to be sweeter tasting than the pole versions. The latter produce the popular big-pod butter beans. Bush limas for the most part don't require staking, although some varieties can grow to twenty-four inches and tend to fall over. Mulching with hay around the plants helps keep the beans off the soil, clean, weed free, and easier to pick.

Shell and dried beans. A staple the world over, shell or dried beans are grown for the seeds inside the pod.

Shell beans are harvested when the pods are fully formed but still somewhat green and soft. Dried beans are allowed to dry on the plants before harvesting. Dried beans can be stored and transported easily and can be used in a wide variety of dishes from soups to salads and main dishes. Shell and dry beans are also available in a number of varieties, often with colorful bean seeds. These include the popular kidney beans used in chili; great northern, the popular soup and main dish bean; navy beans, used in baked beans; the unusual maroon-speckled Jacob's cattle beans; pinto beans for tacos, tamales, and refried beans; black beans for a number of traditional dishes; and horticultural bean, a bean that is often used as a shell bean or when semidry, or can also be dried. We have grown horticulture beans for many years, substituting them for pinto and kidney beans. They're easy to harvest and great as a canned bean. Garbanzo beans may also be used in the green shell or dried. They have a rich nutty flavor, are also called chick peas, and are often served in salad bars. Bush fava beans, also called English broad beans, are green beans used like limas. They are easier to grow in the north than traditional limas.

Edible soybeans have become increasingly popular as a home-garden food and with good reason. They should not be confused with agricultural soybeans, but are eaten by boiling the fresh beans and removing them from the pods. They have an extremely high protein content.

Culture

A. Propagation: direct seeded
B. Amount needed for 100-ft. row: 1 lb.
C. Amount needed for pole plantings: ½ lb.
D. Where to plant: full sun
E. When to plant: After all danger of frost and when soil temperature reaches 60°F
F. Row spacing: 24 in.
G. Pole row spacing: 30 in.
H. Plant spacing in rows: 3 in.
I. Plant spacing in hills: 36 in.
J. Planting depth: 1 in.
K. How much per person in rows: fresh, 10 to 15 ft.; processed, 20 to 30 ft.

L. How much per person in hills: fresh, 3 to 5 hills; processed, 5 to 10 hills

M. Days from planting to eating: bush beans, 50 to 60; pole beans, 70 to 95

Requirements

A. Soil type: Well-drained friable and fertile soil. Work in well-rotted manure or other organic materials before planting.

B. pH: 6.5 to 7.

C. Fertilizer: Avoid high-nitrogen fertilizers as they produce lots of foliage with few pods.

Growing tips. Beans are a warm-season crop and must be planted after all danger of frost has passed and the soil has warmed up to at least 50°F. I prefer the soil to be around 60°F. Poor germination results from planting too quickly in the spring and is especially so with limas. Some companies treat seeds with a fungicide to protect the emerging plants from disease. Untreated seeds should not be planted until the soil is thoroughly warm. As beans are a legume, they benefit from the use of an inoculant.

Some companies offer inoculant, and it can increase production. If you want a continuous summer crop, plant every two to three weeks throughout the summer months. The soil should be well tilled, loose, and friable. Heavy, cloddy soil results in poor germination. Before planting, incorporate about a cup per fifty feet of row of a low-nitrogen fertilizer, such as 5-10-10 or comparable organic fertilizer. Water the fertilizer into the soil and plant the seeds. Beans can be very productive, even just a few plants with the correct care, and it's usually not too much effort to plant a fifty-foot row by hand. I like to overplant and thin to the recommended spacing after germination. You can also use a small mechanical seeder for larger areas. Keep the rows well weeded, and lightly cultivated to keep down weeds, and keep the plants well watered. Side-dress with a complete commercial fertilizer once or twice during the growing season by applying alongside the row and lightly cultivating it in. Once flowering and the pods begin to set, side-dress with one cup of ammonium nitrate (33-0-0) or equivalent nitrogen fertilizer per fifty feet of row. Do not allow the fertilizer to contact the foliage, lightly cultivate, and then water it into the soil. Heavy nitrogen, early on, however, results in lots of foliage with few pods.

Pole beans need lots of support with poles seven- to eight-foot tall. Use poles in tripod fashion, posts with wire or heavy-duty twine strung between them, or A-frame-type supports. The latter can be fastened to a raised bed for efficiently growing pole beans in a small area. Clipping off the ends of the plants when they reach the top creates bushier plants.

Pests. Beans don't have as many pests as some other plants, but a number of beetle varieties can be a problem. Rabbits and deer love the tender young plants and pods.

Harvest. Pick snap beans while the pods are still tender. Older pods can become tough and stringy. Limas and pole beans tend to mature a few at a time, over a longer season, requiring you to pick the beans on the bottom of the plant and work upward as they mature. Pick shell beans, such as horticulture, just when the shell begins to dry but before the beans begin to harden. Pick dried beans after the pods and shells have dried, allowing the beans to dry on the vine.

Storage. For snap beans, pressure can, freeze, or dehydrate. For dried beans, keep cool and dry and away from pests.

***

Beets

Description. Beets belong to the root crop family and are extremely easy to grow, actually one of the easiest crops to grow, as they are bothered by few pests, will grow in a wide range of soil types, and grow relatively fast. Beets are a great choice for raised-bed gardening, and you can grow successive crops for the entire summer, planting about every three weeks. A 4 × 6 foot raised bed can produce more than

⊗ Beets are a root crop and also very easy to grow.

fifty pounds of beets plus the tops, a great choice for small-space gardening. And that's just one planting. Beets are also a very versatile kitchen food. They can be pureed and mashed to be used in soups; oven roasted, simmered, and cooked for Harvard beets; pressure canned; or pickled for the popular beet pickles. Even better yet, beets are good for you. They contain lots of fiber, iron, and folic acid as well as vitamins B_1, C, and A. The tops or greens are even better for you providing vitamins C and A as well as iron.

Types. Beet varieties are available in two types, depending on the shape of the root: globes and cylinders. Beets are also available as early or late maturing.

Culture

A. Propagation: direct seeded or transplanted
B. Amount needed for 100-ft. row: 2 oz.
C. Where to plant: Full sun but do best when temperature of soil and air is slightly cool. Beets do best in the northern portion of the country but can be grown in the south in late winter and early spring.
D. When to plant: Beet seeds will germinate in soil temperatures as low as 40°F. Many growers plant when they plant peas or set out cabbage.
E. Row spacing: 18 in.
F. Plant spacing: 3 in.
G. Depth: ½ in.
H. How much per person: 5- to 10-ft. row fresh, 10- to 20-ft. row processed
I. Days from planting to eating stage: 45 to 65

Requirements

A. Soil type: Soil should be loose and loamy for proper growth of the roots. Hard-packed soils should be built up with compost or well-rotted cow manure. Do not plant in fresh manure.
B. pH: 6.5 to 7
C. Fertilizer: Beets are not heavy feeders. Organic fertilizer, such as well-rotted cow manure, will suffice for most instances; however, application of a water-soluble fertilizer will help create bigger roots. Adding organic fertilizers with potash can also help. Or use 5-10-5 or similar commercial fertilizer.

⊗ It's important to keep beets thinned. Use the thinnings as baby beets and tops for salads.

Growing tips. The two main factors in growing beets are a good, loose soil and a steady, plentiful supply of water throughout the growing season, at least an inch per week. The biggest problem with growing beets is sowing the seeds too close together or not thinning them properly. Beet seeds are actually fruits or a ripened ovary containing several seeds. You'll often get four or more sprouts from each seed. I like to plant about a dozen beet seeds per foot of row, allow them to sprout, and use scissors to cut off all but one sprout from each seed. After the plants have grown for three to four weeks, I thin the plants to about three inches apart. The thinning leaves are delicious in

salads, and the tiny tender beets can be simmered. Soaking the seeds in water overnight will also help germination. For many years I simply planted rows of beets and hoped for the best. Spotty germination, resulting in lots of sprouts in one spot and little or nothing in other areas, led to poor production and lots of weed problems. Then I tried planting beet seeds in my greenhouse at the same time as cabbage and broccoli. Beets transplant very easily, and it's easy to maintain proper spacing. Planted in raised beds in this manner, they're much more productive than direct seeded into rows.

Beets require little in the way of care except weeding and watering. They do not like direct weed competition. A mulch of straw around the plants after thinning helps maintain more even soil temperatures and prevents pale or irregular coloring of the rings (called zoning).

Pests. Beets have very few pests, with leaf miners and some beetles chewing on the leaves.

Harvest. Beets can be harvested any time, and many varieties are grown to produce early "baby beets." The smaller beets, about the size of a

◉ Broccoli belongs to the cabbage family and is highly nutritious. It does take a bit more effort to grow.

golf ball, will be more tender and have better texture and flavor than say softball size. Beets can be left until they get larger, but do not leave much longer than the maturity days on the seed packet, as the plants can get woody or fibrous, especially during hot summer weather. To cook beets, leave about an inch of the tops attached to the unpeeled beet to prevent excessive bleeding.

Storage. Beets can be used fresh, pressure canned, and dehydrated; or late-season or fall beets can be kept in a root cellar or a box filled with moist sand in a cool basement. In areas with mild winter, simply cover the beets with a thick layer of straw for fresh beets anytime.

***

Broccoli

Description. Broccoli belongs to the cabbage family and is one of the most nutritious vegetables. It is very high in vitamins A, B, and C and also provides both calcium and iron. One cooked cup of fresh broccoli is less than fifty calories yet can provide half the minimum daily requirement of A and double the daily requirement for C for an adult. Broccoli is also an excellent source for folic acid, and it is rich in fiber.

Broccoli is not the easiest plant to grow, and it does take space. Broccoli requires the right cool temperatures for proper growth and is very susceptible to insect attacks. Not grown properly, it can be bitter with stunted heads. If you live in an area with no spring and lots of hot weather early in the year, you will do best growing broccoli in the fall. In some areas, you may be able to double crop with both spring and fall crops.

Types. Broccoli is available in a number of varieties, mostly depending on the length to maturity. Two types are available, heading which produces heads like cauliflower and sprouting. Sprouting varieties can produce a continuous crop of sprouts over a longer season, but with smaller heads.

Culture

A. Propagation: direct seeded or transplanted
B. Amount needed for 100-ft. row: ½ oz.
C. Where to plant: direct sun
D. When to plant: early spring, even before last frost if you can cover the plants
E. Row spacing: 30 in.
F. Plant spacing: 24 in.
G. Depth: ½ in.
H. How much per person: fresh, 3 to 5 plants; processed, 5 to 10 plants
I. Days from planting to eating stage: 55 to 70, depending on variety

Requirements

Soil type: A rich loamy soil produces best, but broccoli will grow in less than perfect soils.

pH: Broccoli does not like acidic soils, 6.5 to 7.

Fertilizer: Broccoli is not a heavy feeder. Well-dried cow manure worked into the bed will add to productivity as will occasional fertilizing with a commercial water-soluble fertilizer. Too much nitrogen, however, produces lots of foliage instead of heads.

Growing tips. Broccoli can be direct seeded in the garden or bed, and it is the method often used for producing a fall crop. Broccoli is most often grown from transplants, either plants purchased to set out in March or early April or by starting your own plants indoors. Plant the seeds in a flat in early January, sowing about a half-inch deep. Broccoli plants are easy to grow. I sow tiny rows of seeds in a flat under a light and transplant into plastic trays, paper pots, or foam coffee cups once the plants have two leaves. Keep plants well watered throughout the growing season.

Pests. Treat pests as soon as you spot them. Everything that crawls and flies loves broccoli, but the most common pest and one that causes the most problems is the cabbage worm. Burying inside the head, they're insidiously hard to spot.

Harvest. It's important to harvest broccoli before the buds flower and begin to dry out. Cut off heads so a long stem remains on the plant. With some varieties, numerous side shoots will form. Soak harvested heads in saltwater before eating or preserving if heavily infested with worms.

Storage. Broccoli is best fresh but can also be blanched and frozen for storage.

***

Brussels Sprouts

Description. Brussels sprouts should be called frosty plants because they are primarily a fall crop and actually do best after a light fall frost. A member of the cabbage family, Brussels sprouts are somewhat hard to grow.

Types. Only a few varieties are available, the difference mostly in time to maturity.

Culture

A. Propagation: direct seeded and transplanted

B. Amount needed for 100-ft. row: ½ oz.

C. Where to plant: direct sun

D. When to plant: seed in May, transplant in July for fall crop

E. Row spacing: 24 in.

F. Plant spacing: 12–18 in.

G. Depth: ¼ in.

H. How much per person: fresh, 5 to 6 plants; processed, 5 to 10 plants

I. Days from planting to eating stage: 80 to 100 days

Requirements

A. Soil type: Loamy, rich in organic fertilizer

B. pH: 6.5 to 7

C. Fertilizer: Liquid water soluble or 10-10-10 side-dressed after transplanting

Growing tips. Start seed indoors or in garden in beds in May. Transplant into the garden in July. Keep well watered, weeded, and inspect for pests. Frost improves the flavor of Brussels sprouts.

Pests. It does not have many pests, except for some beetles.

Harvest. Allow buds to remain on plants until after frost and then harvest often, starting with the bottom buds.

Storage. Can be kept in root cellar and cool basement in boxes or does well frozen.

***

Cabbage

Description. A very important crop in many parts of the country, cabbage is a cool-season crop and relatively easy to grow. Cabbage is popular both as a fresh food as well as cooked and added to other dishes. Cabbage is often grown as both a spring and fall crop.

Types. Cabbage is available in both green and red types with several varieties available, as well as in ball or

Cabbage is one of the most important food crops and is an easy grower for the home food garden.

leafy heads. Chinese cabbage is also popular. Another factor in the varieties is the age to maturity. Early-maturing varieties are eaten fresh or frozen. Later-maturing varieties are often grown for winter storage in root cellars. Some varieties are bred to resist diseases from the soil, and some grow better in hotter weather. Most types, however, succumb to disease, pests, and the heads splitting open in the hot weather. For the best cabbage, plant so the heads ripen before hot weather.

Culture

A. Propagation: Spring plantings can be direct seeded, but are usually started indoors and transplanted.

Fall plantings can be started indoors or outdoors in a shady, somewhat-protected area or direct seeded in the beds.

B. Amount needed for 100-ft. row: ¼ to ½ oz.
C. Where to plant: direct sun
D. When to plant: very early spring or in mid- to late summer for a fall crop
E. Row spacing: 24 in.
F. Plant spacing: 12 in
G. Depth: ¼ in
H. How much per person: 3 to 10 plants ball heads, 5 to 10 plants Chinese varieties
I. Days from planting to eating stage: 55 to 105 days

Requirements

A. Soil type: A loose, friable, rich soil
B. pH: 6.5 to 7
C. Fertilizer: Add one pound of complete 12-12-12 or 10-10-10 fertilizer per row before planting or transplanting. Side-dress with a high nitrogen fertilizer after heads begin to form.

Growing tips. Cabbage from transplants is easy to grow, and it's easy to start the seed indoors. This is a good choice for beginning food growers. We start seeds in our greenhouse and transplant. Plan to set out plants in August for a fall crop. Cabbage requires watering throughout the growing season. Several years ago we started growing cabbage in raised beds, and it's easy to keep the plants well weeded and watered, and you can also space them somewhat closer for an intensive gardening situation.

Pests. Cabbage worms, cabbage butterfly, looper worms or inch worms, imported cabbage worms are some of the worst pests. Sevin dust will keep them under control. Wood ashes are an organic remedy.

Harvest. Harvest heads after they firm up but before they split and, if you're not into pesticides, before the bugs get to them.

Storage. Early varieties can be kept refrigerated to use fresh, frozen, or made into sauerkraut. Later varieties can be kept in a cool storage area or even covered with straw and kept in the garden in some areas.

***

Cauliflower

Description. Cauliflower is a popular vegetable many gardeners try to

grow, but it's a bit more difficult to grow properly than many other vegetables, including its cousin broccoli. Cauliflower is a cool-season crop and must be started and planted very early in order to grow the heads. Once hot weather hits, cauliflower stops producing. You may be better off growing as a cool-season, fall crop. Cauliflower is rich in iron and vitamin C.

Types. Cauliflower varieties are relatively few in number. The biggest difference is in its time to mature. Shorter-maturing varieties are best for the south, but the heads are usually smaller as well. Colored varieties rather than the white heads are also available. Some "self-blanching" varieties are also available.

Culture

A. Propagation: By direct seeding or transplanting. Starting indoors and transplanting is usually the best method.
B. Amount needed for 100-ft. row: ¼ oz.
C. Where to plant: full sun
D. When to plant: early spring or late summer for fall crop in some areas
E. Row spacing: 24 in.
F. Plant spacing: 24 in.
G. Depth: ¼ in.
H. How much per person: fresh, 5 plants; processed, 10 plants
I. Days from planting to eating stage: 65 to 70

Requirements

A. Soil type: rich, loose with full sun and good drainage
B. pH: 6 to 7
C. Fertilizer: High in nitrogen with trace elements of boron. Lack of nitrogen can cause the heads to

be stunted and yellowed. In order to produce, cauliflower must grow fast. Soil must be rich in organic fertilizer. Use a general-purpose fertilizer before planting and then add nitrogen as the heads begin to fill. If the pH is low, add lime. Alkaline soils can prevent the plants from absorbing boron, an important mineral for cauliflower. Granite dust and rock phosphate are good sources of boron.

Growing tips. The best method in most instances is to start the seeds indoors eight weeks before the last frost date for your area. This should create transplants ready to set out from two to three weeks before the last frost date. For a fall crop, sow seeds in pots twelve weeks before the first fall frost. Set out plants when they have three leaves and a small bud in the center, which will form the head. When transplanting, make sure the soil around the plant is thoroughly soaked and the plants are well settled. As the plant grows, the leaves tend to curl away from the heads. When the heads are about two inches in size, the heads are shielded from the sun by pulling the leaves up and tying them around the head with a soft cloth or string.

Pests. Cabbage worms can be a problem.

Harvest. It's best to harvest cauliflower earlier than later, as the heads tend to become loose and lose their white color. This is usually when the heads are four to six inches in diameter and the curds are still compact. Cut off the heads with a sharp knife, leaving the inner layer of leaves around the head.

Storage. Cauliflower is best eaten while fresh, but a bountiful crop can be blanched and frozen.

***

Carrots

Description. Rich in vitamin A and beta-carotene, carrots are one of the most common vegetables, as well as one of the most beneficial and nutritious. Carrots are cool-season root crops that grow almost anywhere, but require loose, porous soil.

Types. Carrots are available in several varieties mostly dependent on the size and shape of the root. Sturdy, blocky varieties yield more pounds per row and are the best choices for canning and storing. The more slender varieties are best for eating fresh.

Culture

A. Propagation: direct seeded
B. Amount needed for 100-ft. row: ¼ to ½ oz. depending on variety
C. Where to plant: full sun
D. When to plant: Early spring with successive plantings through spring. Late summer for fall crop in some areas. Carrots do not germinate well in hot weather.

E. Row spacing: 18 in.
F. Plant spacing: 3 in.
G. Depth: ¼ in.
H. How much per person: fresh, 5 to 10 ft.; processed, 10 to 15 ft.
I. Days from planting to eating stage: 75 to 80

Requirements

A. Soil type: rich and loose with full sun, good drainage, and no rocks
B. pH: 6.5 to 7.0
C. Fertilizer: general-purpose

Growing tips. Make sure the ground is well pulverized and loose, not clay or cloddy. Rocks, roots, and other objects can cause the carrots to split. Adding some sand may help as can a big dose of compost. Before working the soil, add two pounds of complete fertilizer per one-hundred-foot row and work well into the soil. Do not use fresh manure, as it can make the carrots tough. Plant as early as you can work the soil in the spring. As carrots are slow to germinate, add a few radishes to help mark the rows. Once stalks appear, side-dress with one pound of high nitrogen fertilizer per one-hundred-foot row. Keep well weeded and keep the crowns covered to prevent the root tops from turning green. Mulching can be a great help in keeping down weeds and lightly protecting the tops.

Pests. Carrots are troubled by few pests and diseases, and wireworms can be a problem. Sprinkle wood ashes along the rows for protection.

Harvest. Harvest as soon as you like with the first tender, juicy baby carrots. For a general crop, wait until after the first frost, then dig, and store or process.

Storage. Carrots can be stored in several ways—pressure canned, frozen, dehydrated, or even in the old-time root cellar or in a cool, moist area with temperature from just above freezing to about 43°F and with a fairly high humidity of 90 to 95 percent. One old-time method was the root barrel, using a barrel or large bucket. Fill the container with carrots and then fill the mouth of the barrel with straw or hay. Bury the barrel in a trench on its side and cover with straw or hay and then add a thin layer of soil. Add more straw and a thicker layer of soil.

***

⊘ Many crops, such as carrots, can be stored in an old-fashioned root cellar.

Swiss Chard

Description. Swiss chard is actually a variety of beet but without the root. The tops look much the same as beets and the fine-textured leaves are often used like spinach. Swiss chard is easy to grow, does well in hot weather, even droughty conditions, and is often substituted for spinach in hot climates. It is not only rich in vitamin A, but it also adds "decor" to your garden. Swiss chard can be grown early in spring as a cool-season plant and also does well as a fall planting. If covered with a thick layer of straw mulch, it will keep producing throughout the winter in some areas.

Types. Swiss chard is available in two types, red veined or white veined, and several varieties.

Culture

A. Propagation: direct seeded or transplanted
B. Amount needed for 100-ft. row: 2 oz.
C. Where to plant: full sun
D. When to plant: 2 to 4 weeks before last frost date
E. Row spacing: 18 in.
F. Plant spacing: 3 to 6 in.
G. Depth: ½ in.
H. How much per person: fresh, 5 to 10 ft.; processed, 10 to 15 ft.
I. Days from planting to eating stage: 55 to 65

Requirements

A. Soil type: any loose, good soil
B. pH: It does not do well in acid soil.

❤ Swiss chard is another easy-grower and can be grown in spring or fall.

C. Fertilizer: Side-dress with nitrogen fertilizer after plants are well started.

Growing tips. Swiss chard grows fairly prolifically, even throughout the summer. Successive plantings are not usually required, although some gardeners may wish to make a fall planting. About the only requirement is to keep the plants well watered and weeded or mulched.

Pests. It has few pests.

Harvest. Harvest the outer or first most-tender leaves, usually in a couple of months. Leave the inner leaves to develop for a continuous harvest.

Storage. Quite often used fresh but may also be frozen like spinach.

***

Collards

Description. Primarily known as a southern green, collards can also be grown in the north since they withstand both heat and cold quite well. They grow and taste similar to cabbage but do not form heads. Collards are rich in both vitamins B and C. In many areas, they do best as a fall and winter crop.

Types. Not a lot of varieties are available, and seeds are not as available from as many seed companies.

Culture

A. Propagation: direct seeded or transplanted
B. Amount needed for 100-ft. row: ½ oz.
C. Where to plant: direct sun
D. When to plant: Early spring, even before last frost if you can cover the plants.
E. Row spacing: 24 in.
F. Plant spacing: 12 in.
G. Depth: ¼ in.
H. How much per person per year: fresh, 5 to 10 ft.; processed, 10 to 15 ft.
I. Days from planting to eating stage: 85 to 95

Requirements

A. Soil type: A loose, friable, rich soil. Adding well-rotted manure or compost can be a great help.
B. pH: 6.5 to 7.0
C. Fertilizer: Add 1 lb. of complete 12-12-12 or 10-10-10 fertilizer per row before planting or setting out. Fertilize during midseason with 1 pound of 12-12-12 per row.

Growing tips. Grow as for cabbage starting seeds indoors or direct seeding. Make sure to keep well watered during hot, dry weather. Weeds can be a problem. Keep the plants well cultivated and weeded. Mulching can help cut down on weeds. Flavor improves after a light frost.

Pests. It has few pests.

Harvest. The young plants can be used whole, although the most common tactic is to remove the tender top leaves, especially as the plant matures.

Storage. The tender leaves can be blanched and frozen following directions for spinach.

***

❂ Sweet corn is a garden favorite, but it does take space and some effort in growing.

Corn

Description. Sweet corn is from the grass family, and it is a true Native American plant. In fact, the Native Americans taught the first immigrants to grow this valuable food. It is fairly easy to grow and extremely popular. Sweet corn does require quite a bit of space, rich soil, lots of fertilizer and water, and some effort. The Native Americans planted corn in hills or groups of seed with a dead fish placed alongside the hole as fertilizer. The

taste of homegrown fresh corn makes it well worth the effort.

Choosing sweet corn can be confusing. First, sweet corn is classified according to the colors of the kernels. It is available as yellow, white, and bicolor. Bicolor corn usually has about 20 percent white and 80 percent yellow kernels. In addition, sweet corn is available as open pollinated or hybrid. Open-pollinated or heritage varieties have withstood the test of time and still produce lots of corn, especially for market growers or preserving. For the most part, heritage varieties are hardier than hybrids and include such favorites as country gentleman, Stowell's evergreen, and golden bantam, popular corn for over one hundred years. Hybrid sweet corn varieties have been bred to produce specific traits, and a wide variety exists, mostly concerning the sugar content. The package or catalog describes the types. These different types have different cultural requirements.

Types

A. su

These are a normal sweet corn with a firm yet creamy texture. Varieties have differing levels of sugar content (9–16 percent). The sugars of this type convert quite rapidly to starch after harvest, so the varieties must be consumed quickly or processed after harvest. This is the oldest type of hybrid and produces a hearty corn with vigorous germination and is easy to grow. It must be isolated (250 to 300 ft. or by three-plus weeks in maturity) from sh2 varieties.

B. se, se+, or EH

These sugar-enhanced varieties produce an increased tenderness and sweetness. The conversion from sugar to starch is slower, so they keep longer once picked. Some se+ varieties can last up to two weeks before converting to starch and becoming tougher. Some varieties do not have to be isolated; some must be isolated from sh2 and su varieties.

C. sh2

These corn varieties are called supersweet or Xtra sweet. The su gene (short for shrunken) creates a corn with very high sugar content (28–44 percent) that is very slow to convert to starch and with a greatly increased sweetness. This corn has extrasweet flavor and crispness. The seeds or dry kernels of this type are very small and shriveled up.

Culture

A. Propagation: direct seeded
B. Amount needed for 100-ft. row: ¼ lb.
C. Where to plant: Corn does best in areas with lots of hot, summer sun, although some varieties can be planted in cooler climates.

The area chosen for a corn patch should have at least 8 to 10 hours of full sunlight.

D. When to plant: Soil temperature of at least 60°F and 7 to 10 days after last predicted frost or, better yet, later.

E. Row spacing: 36 in.

F. Plant spacing: 10 to 12 in.

G. Depth: ½ in.

H. How much per person per year: fresh, 15 to 25 ft; processed, 30 to 50 ft.

I. Days from planting to eating stage: 70 to 85

Requirements

Soil type: rich, loose with full sun and good drainage

pH: 6.0 to 6.5

Fertilizer: Requires high-nitrogen fertilizer. Purchased high-nitrogen fertilizers may be used or cottonseed meal or well-dried manure.

Growing tips. Corn is very sensitive to cool weather. Most corn packets suggest waiting until the soil temperature is at least 60°F, and in many areas this will work, as long as there isn't a late frost. I prefer to wait until soil temperature is at least 70°F and at least a week after the last predicted killing frost. We usually plant corn the first week of May in the Missouri Ozarks where we live. Corn planted too early will simply rot in the ground and not sprout. The Xtra sweet varieties require extremely warm soil. Faster growing, early corn you plant earlier and take your chances. In some areas, with late springs and short growing seasons, one solution is to cover the soil with black plastic and allow it to warm the soil. Then punch holes in the plastic and plant corn. If you want to put up corn for the winter, plant a single late-spring crop to ripen all at once. It does take quite a bit of space to plant a corn patch providing food to process, about a thirty- to fifty-foot row per person. Corn should also be spaced a minimum of thirty-six inches apart, so you're looking at about a 15 × 50 foot area for a family of four. Many varieties will stay sweet in the refrigerator for ten days to two weeks, providing lots of fresh corn on the cob. If you wish to extend your roasting-ear season, plant successive crops, spaced two to three weeks apart, or plant varieties with different maturity dates. But watch mixing the super sweets, as they should be isolated by at least five hundred feet.

Corn may be planted in rows or in hills or seed groups. In the latter, three to four seeds are planted every fifteen inches. I prefer to plant in rows. You can plant corn in a more intensive spacing, even as close as twenty-four-inch rows, but it requires more work in weeding. I also plant corn closer than the packets suggest, about four inches apart, and then thin the plants to about eight inches. Closer spacing usually results in only one ear per stalk while wide spacing two ears per stalk. Corn is a monoecious with the plant having both male and female flowers on each stalk. The tassel at the top is the male flower, with the silks the female flower. The silks protruding from the top of the cob are actually hollow tubes leading to what will be a kernel of corn. Pollination is by wind, and the pollen from the male flower must land on each silk to produce a full ear. Ears only partially filled are due to poor pollination. One major cause of poor pollination is a windstorm that blows the stalks from their upright position. Another reason is the planting pattern. Corn should not be planted in a single or double long row, but in blocks of at least three and preferably more rows in order to provide proper pollination.

The soil should be well worked to a depth of at least eight inches with a tiller, working in compost or well-rotted manure. One secret to adding organic nitrogen is to alternate the corn patch with a legume such as a bean or pea patch, as these plants add nitrogen to the soil. Another old-time method is to plant a legume such as clover in the fall and then turn it under in early spring. The best planting is on a finely worked soil, so don't till or work the soil during wet weather to keep from creating clods. Planting a large corn patch by hand takes quite a bit of work, laying out the rows with a string line, creating the furrow with a hoe, dropping the seed, and covering with a rake. A small hand-pushed mechanical planter can make this chore much easier and faster.

A soil test should be done and followed for the best corn crop. Without a soil test, a standard practice is to use six pounds of 10-10-10 or five pounds of 12-12-12 fertilizer per one hundred feet of row. Lay out the rows and spread this before planting the seed. For the ultimate corn patch, the plants should be side-dressed with a high-nitrogen fertilizer two to three times during the season, once when the plants are about six inches high, just before the plants begin to tassel and when the plants are in full tassel with silks exposed. To side-dress, dig a shallow furrow near the row, add the fertilizer and cover, but be careful not to cut into the stalk roots. In the past, ammonium nitrate (34-0-0) has been the most common commercial fertilizer used by home gardeners, or you can use the organic cottonseed meal fertilizer.

Cultivate shallowly to remove weeds but, again, be careful not to damage the root system. Hoeing a small mound of soil up around the roots can help protect stalks from wind damage. Small patches can be mulched to control weeds and help contain moisture. Water, water, and more water are needed to grow corn— the reason irrigated farm corn does the best. Provide a minimum of one inch of water per week, and this is especially important during pollination and ear development. It's important to water in the early morning or by early afternoon to allow the foliage to dry before dark. One excellent method of watering corn is to use soaker hoses placed alongside the rows. I usually place one hose in the patch, pulling it out and moving it to the next row once each row is thoroughly soaked.

Pests. The corn earworm is the most common pest. Placing a drop of mineral oil in each ear just as it begins to tassel can help. Other pests include the following: aphids, flea beetles, cutworms, seed-corn maggots, southern corn rootworm, wireworms, fall armyworms, European corn borers, and Japanese beetles.

Harvest. Best picked at the milk stage or when a milky juice squirts out when the kernels are pierced with a thumbnail. The ears should easily snap off the stalk.

Storage: Best eaten immediately, but some varieties will store for several days, even a week or so in a refrigerator. Pressure can, freeze, or dehydrate the cut-off kernels. Dent or field corn grains can be dried on the plant and then ground into meal for storage.

***

Cucumber

Description: Cucumbers are a delightfully easy vegetable to grow, and they provide both fresh cucumbers for salads and other summer dishes, but they are also processed to produce a wide variety of pickles. Cucumbers fresh from your garden resemble nothing like the waxed kind often found in grocery stores.

Types. A wide range of varieties are available, including the popular burpless types, big, small, long, and short.

Culture

A. Propagation: direct seeded
B. Amount needed for 100-ft. row: ¼ oz.
C. Where to plant: direct sun
D. When to plant: late spring, well after frost danger
E. Row spacing: 36 in.
F. Plant spacing: 48 in.

⊗ Cucumbers are easy to grow and are a must for garnishing summer salads.

G. Depth: ½ in.
H. How much per person: fresh, 2 to 3 hills; processed, 3 to 6 hills
I. Days from planting to eating stage: 65 to 70

Requirements

Soil type: a rich, deep soil
pH: 6.5 to 7.0
Fertilizer: a general-purpose fertilizer, chemical, or organic

Growing tips. Cucumbers need lots of water and lots of fertilizer. In most instances, cucumbers are grown in hills rather than rows, unless you're market gardening. You'll usually get fifteen to thirty seeds of many hybrids and one hundred or more seeds of most standard varieties in a packet. Space hills about five feet apart. Dig deep holes where the hills will be. Fill in the hole with plenty of well-rotted manure or compost. Then add about three inches of garden soil to create the hill. Place about five to six seeds to a hill. Cultivate shallowly until the vines begin to grow. Heavy mulch can prevent a lot of weeding problems, but it will take quite a bit to mulch the entire space. Cucumbers do extremely well grown on trellises or vertically, and they don't take up nearly as much space. Growing on black plastic keeps down the weeds, but they take up a lot of garden space in this manner. My cucumber tactics have been refined over a number of years, growing them more intensively. I have a permanent trellis made from a section of cattle panel supported by steel posts and centered in a raised bed. I plant three hills on each side of the fifteen-foot panel, spacing closer than conventional spacing. As soon as the plants are up, I mulch the bed heavily. Cucumbers need lots of water as well as food. The latter can be in the form of chemical or organic fertilizer, using a general fertilizer mix. My method is even simpler. I bury a plastic food container, with the bottom perforated, in the center of the hill and plant the seeds around the container. Once a day during the growing season, I fill the containers with water. About once a week, I fill the containers with manure tea. Any liquid fertilizer will do.

Pests. There are lots of bugs and beetles that like cucumber plants, especially the striped cucumber beetle. Remove by hand or shake on Sevin dust or wood ashes.

⊗ Eggplant is both a decorative and edible food plant.

Harvest. Harvest cucumbers for slicing and salads when they're about medium size and while they're still dark green. For pickling, harvest the cucumbers while they're still fairly small. Regardless, keep picking, usually every other day. Allowing old cucumbers to stay on the vine reduces the yield.

Storage. Store for short periods in perforated bags in the refrigerator. Preserve as pickles.

***

Eggplant

Description. Eggplants are a semitropical plant used in many Mediterranean dishes. It has beautiful purple flowers and glossy black fruits. These plants provide not only a bit of decor to your garden but can also be grown as a tasty "ornament," intermingled with flowers in containers on your deck or patio. Eggplants are extremely sensitive to cold.

Types. Several varieties are available, mostly depending on size of the fruits and days to maturity.

Culture

A. Propagation: transplanted
B. Amount needed for 100-ft. row: ½ oz.
C. Where to plant: direct sun to partial shade (young plants need some shade)
D. When to plant: late spring (1 to 2 weeks after danger of frost)
E. Row spacing: 24 in.
F. Plant spacing: 24 in.
G. Depth: 2 to 3 in.
H. How much per person per year: 2 to 3 plants
I. Days from planting to eating stage: 80 to 90

Requirements

Soil type: rich, loamy
pH: 6.5 to 7.0
Fertilizer: general-purpose, side-dress with a good general-purpose

Growing tips. Make sure the transplants are well hardened and set out after all danger of frost. Mulching heavily keeps the ground cool and moist, a must for eggplant.

Pests. Lots of bugs like eggplant, including the potato bug.

Harvest. Harvest when fruits are fully grown, but still bright in color.

Storage. It will not store well, even in a refrigerator.

***

Garlic

Description. A flavorful vegetable utilized in many dishes, garlic is easy to grow and is grown in much the same manner as onions. Garlic is good for you, with chemical compounds that are said to help lower blood pressure and reduce the risks of heart disease and cancer.

Types. Several varieties are available, some for southern and some for northern growers.

Culture

A. Propagation: setting out bulbs
B. Amount needed for 100-ft. row: 4 lbs.
C. Where to plant: direct sun
D. When to plant: spring or fall
E. Row spacing: 18 in.
F. Plant spacing: 8 to 10 in.
G. Depth: 1 to 2 in.
H. How much per person per year: 1 lb.
I. Days from planting to eating stage: 6 mos.

Requirements

Soil type: deep, fertile
pH 6.57
Fertilizer: general-purpose, side-dress with general-purpose

Growing tips. Garlic can be planted in early spring for harvest in August, or it can be planted in the fall for harvest in the spring. The latter method produces bigger bulbs. Plant and fertilize in the same manner as for onions. Garlic does best, especially when fall planted, in raised beds. Intermingle with onions when spring planting. Keep well mulched, especially important if fall planting and overwintering.

Pests. It has few pests.

Harvest. Harvest when bulbs are big enough to use.

Storage. Can be dried and kept in mesh bags or braided as with onions.

***

Kale

Description. Although kale doesn't form a head, it's thought to be a form of cabbage. Kale can be grown almost anywhere in spring or fall and is easy to grow. It is most often planted as a fall crop and will even overwinter in some areas of mild freezing. Kale is high in vitamin A and makes a great winter green and substitute for cabbage. Like turnips, the flavor is improved by a frost.

Types. Its varieties are somewhat limited.

Culture

A. Propagation: direct seeded or transplanted
B. Amount needed for 100-ft. row: ½ oz.
C. Where to plant: full sun
D. When to plant: mid- to late summer, depending on the locale
E. Row spacing: 24 in.
F. Plant spacing: 8 in.
G. Depth: ¼ in.
H. How much per person: fresh, 5 to 10 ft.; processed, 10 to 15 ft.
I. Days from planting to eating stage: 50 to 65

Requirements

Soil type: A deep loamy soil. It doesn't do well in heavy-clay soils.

pH: 6.5 to 7.0

Fertilizer: Apply general fertilizer before seeding.

Growing tips. Kale can be seeded successively about two weeks apart for a continuous harvest.

Pests. It has few pests.

Harvest. Harvest after a frost, cutting away the outer leaves. Or cut entire plant and use only the tender inner leaves.

Storage. May be kept in perforated plastic bags in refrigerator for a couple of weeks. Blanch and freeze excess to be used like cooked cabbage.

***

Kohlrabi

Description. What a strange vegetable kohlrabi is. Unusual looking and with a somewhat strange taste, kohlrabi resembles a turnip, and it has become increasingly popular. Kohlrabi can be grown both as a spring and fall crop, although it grows best in cool weather. Kohlrabi is delicious when cooked or fresh and is high in vitamin C. Hot weather tends to make the roots somewhat bitter.

C. Where to plant: full sun
D. When to plant: early spring or late summer
E. Row spacing: 24 in.
F. Plant spacing: 4 in.
G. Depth: ¼ in.
H. How much per person: fresh, 3 to 5 ft.
I. Days from planting to eating stage: 55 to 65

Requirements

Soil type: Kohlrabi is fairly easy to grow, requiring only a rich organic soil with no stones, although the root grows primarily out of the ground.

pH: 6.5 to 7.0

Fertilizer: all-purpose

Growing tips. Keep well watered and weeded or mulched.

Pests. It has few pests.

Harvest. Pull the bulbs when they're about one and a half to two inches in diameter. As they get bigger, they become tougher and somewhat bitter.

Storage. Use fresh or store in a cool, dry place such as a root cellar.

Types. Not a lot of varieties are available of this strange plant. Most are white skinned, but purple varieties are also available.

Culture

A. Propagation: direct seeded
B. Amount needed for 100-ft. row: ¼ oz.

★★★

⊗ Growing your own lettuce for a summer salad is easy, even for first-timers. Lettuce is available in several varieties. Above is one type of lettuce.

Lettuce

Description. Lettuce is one of the easiest foods to grow and one of the most popular. Lettuce can be grown in a garden, in a container, even in a greenhouse for winter-long salads. It's also good for you because it has lots of vitamin A. Lettuce can be sown for successive crops in both spring and summer, but it does not do well in extremely hot weather.

Types. A wide variety of lettuce is available. Part of the fun of growing your own is growing several different varieties to produce colorful and flavorful salads. Lettuce is divided into four varieties. Three varieties are popular with home food growers. Loose-leaf or nonheading varieties have a loose leaf and rounded or rosette shape. They are the easiest to grow and are available in both green and red types. Butterheads are

⊗ Above is romaine lettuce.

a semiheading type with loosely folding leaves. They are also easy to grow. Cos or romaine, the continental lettuce, has tall upright, loosely formed heads with a unique flavor. They're easy to grow and do better in hot weather than other types. Most are self-blanching, but tying the outer leaves together can produce a more delicate flavor. The last types are the cabbage heads. These are the lettuce heads found at the supermarket. They do not do well in hot weather and can be a challenge in some areas for the

home food grower to produce, especially to produce the big heads that are commercially grown.

Culture

A. Propagation: direct seeded or transplanted
B. Amount needed for 100-ft. row: ¼ oz.
C. Where to plant: direct sun
D. When to plant: 2 weeks before average date of last frost
E. Row spacing: 18 in.
F. Plant spacing: 2 in.
G. Depth: ¼ in.
H. How much per person: 5 to 10 ft. per year
I. Days from planting to eating stage: 35 to 50

Requirements

A. Soil type: any good, well-drained garden soil
B. pH: 6.75. It does not do well in acid soil.
C. Fertilizer: a light application of complete fertilizer at planting or seeding time

Growing tips. You've got to beat the heat to grow lettuce. One method is to start seeds indoors and transplant just after the last frost. Both romaine and butterhead varieties do well started indoors; loose leaf can also be started but is usually so fast growing it's best direct seeded. Sow at ten-day intervals for a continued spring or early-summer crop. Lettuce is somewhat slow to germinate, especially during cold or cool weather, so when sowing directly into the garden, sprinkle a few radish seeds along with the lettuce. Keep well watered. Lettuce is also a great plant for growing in raised beds or even in patio planters.

Pests. Lettuce doesn't have many pests, as it usually grows fairly fast.

Harvest. Lettuce may be harvested in several ways. The most common method is to remove the outer leaves as soon as they become large enough to eat. This is the best tactic with leaf lettuce. Another method is to thin the plants and allow them to form compact heads and then harvest the entire plant. Romaine and butterheads do well with this method. Another method is to use scissors to clip off the tops of the plant. The plant will regrow leaves.

Storage. Lettuce can be kept for several days in a refrigerator in perforated plastic bags. Or wrap the clean damp leaves in a damp towel and place in the refrigerator. If picked and cleaned in the morning, the leaves will be crisp for an evening salad.

***

Leeks

Description: Milder in flavor but similar to onions, leeks are a very popular gourmet vegetable, adding a European taste to any number

⊗ Summer salads, such as lettuce and spinach, do well in raised beds.

of dishes. Leeks do not bulb as do onions.

Types. Varieties are somewhat limited.

Culture

A. Propagation: direct seeded or can be started indoors for transplanting as bunches
B. Amount needed for 100-ft. row: 1 oz.
C. Where to plant: direct sun
D. When to plant: indoors, 8 weeks before outdoor planting time; outdoors, early spring
E. Row spacing: 18 in.
F. Plant spacing: 3 in.
G. Depth: ½ in.
H. How much per person: fresh, 10 to 15 ft.
I. Days from planting to eating stage: 130 days

Requirements

Soil type: Leeks require a rich deep loamy soil. They grow best in raised beds.

pH: 6.5 to 7.0

Fertilizer: Leeks require lots of nitrogen for good growth, especially during the early stages of their growth.

Growing tips. Leeks are available both as seeds and as plants in bunches to be set out. Plant as you would onions. Leeks, however, are not day-length sensitive, and their tops do not fall over. Sow in shallow trenches. Keep the plants well watered and side-dress with nitrogen during the growing season. Leeks do not like competition, so keep them well weeded and watered. Hilling up the soil from the sides of the trenches around the plants about six to eight inches blanches the lower stems and keeps them white. Deep mulch can also be used for the same purpose.

Pests. As with onions, there are few pests except the onion maggot.

Harvest. Harvest as soon as the stalks mature.

Storage. Most commonly used fresh but can be stored in perforated plastic bags in the refrigerator for a short period of time.

***

Melons

Description. The melons, honeydew, and muskmelon, also known as cantaloupe, are popular especially as breakfast foods. They provide a lot of

⊗ Melons, such as cantaloupes, muskmelons, and honeydews, take up a lot of garden space, but the homegrown taste can't be beat.

C. Where to plant: direct sun
D. When to plant: late spring after all chance of frost
E. Row spacing: 48 in.
F. Plant spacing: 60 in.
G. Depth: ½ in.
H. How much per person: 3 to 5 hills
I. Days from planting to eating stage: 80 to 90

fiber in addition to their great tastes. Cantaloupes have a netted skin and more of an aroma than muskmelons. Growing your own melons takes quite a bit of space and effort. Melons also require a long growing season. Any cool weather can easily injure melons.

Types. A wide variety of cantaloupes, muskmelons, and honeydew or green-fleshed melons is available.

Culture

A. Propagation: direct seeded or transplanted
B. Amount needed for 100-ft. row: ¼ oz.

Requirements

Soil type: rich sandy soil
pH: 6.5 to 7.0
Fertilizer: all-around general-purpose

Growing tips. Because of the long growing season, transplants are often the best choice for some areas. The plants, however, must be transplanted with care, as they don't like their roots disturbed. Plant seeds indoors in peat pots or newspaper pots. If you have a long growing season, direct seed in hills. Hills should be spaced about six feet apart. Dig deep holes and add some coarse sand and compost as well as well-rotted manure. I like to place a plastic container with holes in the bottom in each hill. Bring the hill up around the container with compost or rich garden soil and plant eight to ten seeds per hill. Keep lightly cultivated until the seedlings are up. Then thin to just four of the best plants and mulch heavily. I have a permanent melon patch covered with black plastic. This prevents having to weed, keeps the soil warmer for earlier starts, and actually creates miniature raised beds. I never walk on the areas that grow the plants, so there is no compaction. Merely dig the hills over and refill with humus and fertilizer each year. Melons need lots of water and food. The containers allow for easy watering and feeding of the plants.

Pests. Melons have lots of pests, including the cucumber beetle.

Harvest. Harvest when the fruits come off easily from the stem. Lift up the melon; if it's ripe, it will come off easily.

Storage. Store in the refrigerator. Cut into balls or cubes, place in a light sugar and water syrup, and freeze for winter use.

★★★

Okra

Description. Also called gumbo, the pods are used mostly in soups, adding flavor and thickening the soup. They're a very important ingredient of the Louisiana Cajun dish called gumbo. Okra is also popular breaded and fried.

Types. A number of varieties of this unusual plant are available, mostly depending on size. Smaller sizes are available for container or pot growing.

Culture

A. Propagation: direct seeded or transplanted

B Amount needed for 100-ft. row: 1 oz.

C. Where to plant: direct sun

D. When to plant: direct seed or transplant after all danger of frost

E. Row spacing: 30 in.

F. Plant spacing: 12 in.

G. Depth: ½ in.

H. How much per person: fresh, 3 to 5 ft.; processed, 5 to 10 ft.

I. Days from planting to eating stage: 55 to 60

Requirements

Soil type: rich, deep, and fertile

pH: 7.0 to 7.5

Fertilizer: high nitrogen

Growing tips. As you can guess, this plant does best in hot weather. Wait at least a couple of weeks after your last frost or when the soil temperature reaches at least 70°F. For direct seeding, sow seeds one inch apart and then thin to eighteen inches apart once the seedlings are well up. For transplants, use paper or peat pots, as okra doesn't do well when the roots are disturbed. Soak the seeds overnight in warm water to increase germination. Okra must have deep, loose, and friable soil down to at least eight to ten inches. Use plenty of compost and dried manure to create a rich, deep soil. Okra is also a heavy feeder, especially of nitrogen. Side-dress with nitrogen as well.

Pests. Okra has few pests.

Harvest. Harvest the pods when they're about two to three inches in length. As they continue to grow and mature, they become tough and stringy.

Storage. Store in plastic bags in the warmest part of your refrigerator. Freeze for future use or bread and freeze for fried okra.

***

Onions

Description. Another "easy grow" for the first-timers, onions are also one of the most popular plants with all gardeners. Although easy to grow, successfully growing onions can be somewhat confusing because they can be grown from seed, sets, and transplants or bunches. And if that wasn't enough, onions also come as

❮❮ Onions are also easy to grow and do well in beds.

❮❮ Onions are available as seed, bulbs, or transplants.

winter or self-seeding onions. Onions are good for you, as they are packed with compounds said to reduce risks from cancer and heart disease.

Types. A wide range of types as well as varieties of onions are available including the following: sweet and keeper. Onions grow in two stages—the first stage is immediately after planting when all the energy is directed to growing the green tops. The second stage, the forming of the bulb, begins after the tops are well established. The length of day and sunlight has a direct effect on the formation of the bulb. Onion bulbs or varieties are available in three types: long day, short day, and neutral. Long-day onions need from thirteen to sixteen hours of sunlight per day and do best in the north. Short-day onions do best in the south. Day-neutral onions can be successfully grown anywhere.

Perennial, Egyptian, or winter onions are a totally different story, and they also definitely have a place in the garden. They can provide green onions or scallions during the year when regular onions are not producing. They're actually not perennials, but direct-seed themselves with tiny bulblets at the end of the growing season.

In late summer, the tiny bulbs form on the top of the mother plant. If left as is, they will fall over and reseed themselves, producing green onions by fall. They will overwinter as is in some locales, or light mulch will help keep them through the winter in colder climates. You can pull off the tiny bulbs and plant them in the fall but do not store them to plant in the spring, as they tend to dry out.

Culture

A. Propagation: seed, sets, transplants
B. Amount needed for 100-ft. row: ½ oz.
C. Where to plant: direct sun
D. When to plant: early spring
E. Row spacing: 18 in.
F. Plant spacing: 3 in.
G. Depth: ¼ in.
H. How much per person: 25 to 50 ft.
I. Days from planting to eating stage: 100 to 120

◈ Onions come in a variety of colors, like white, yellow, and red.

Requirements

A. Soil type: loose, friable, rich, and well drained
B. pH: 7.0 to 7.5
C. Fertilizer: Use fertilizers high in phosphorus and potash as well as use well-rotted manure and compost to create a fertile deep bed.

Growing tips. Although onions are commonly grown in rows, I prefer to grow them in raised-bed boxes. One of the main reasons is the soil isn't compacted, and I can apply the correct mix of fertilizer for good growth. Onions do their best green growth in cool weather, so get them in the garden as soon as the soil can be worked. I typically plant both sets and bunches. The sets are placed equidistant three inches apart. Pick through the sets to obtain bulbs at least one-half inch in diameter. Smaller bulbs will not produce large onions. Plant the bulbs

⊗ Perennial or Egyptian onions can produce scallions during winter and early spring seasons.

one-half-inch deep. Bunches, which I usually use as scallions or green onions, are planted thickly in rows and then thinned as they grow. I use the thinnings as green onions. Onions do not like competition. It's important to keep them well weeded using shallow

⊗ Onions are pulled when the tops fall over, are allowed to dry, and then can be braided in strings.

cultivation or by hand-pulling weeds. Since onions are shallow rooted, they must be kept well watered. Mulch can also be a great help in growing onions, especially in raised beds.

Onions can also be grown from seeds. Although it takes more time and effort, more seed varieties are available than with bunches or sets. Plant seeds for transplant onions indoors at least twelve weeks before transplanting time. Treat as with any other indoor seeded plant.

Pests. One of the most common pests is the onion maggot. Planting radishes in with the onions can help remedy the problem, as the maggots prefer the radishes to the onions.

Harvest. Harvest when the tops fall down. Throw into windrows and allow them to cure for two to three days. Protect from rain and sunscald with light shade if necessary. Do not wait until the cool, wet days of fall, as the plants may begin a second growth and will not keep as well.

Storage. After the bulbs are dry, store in mesh bags, slatted crates, or by braiding into strings. Ideal temperature for storage and long keeping is 40° to 45°F.

***

Peas

Description. Peas are another garden tradition. They take a bit of effort to grow but are great canned or frozen. You can't beat fresh-out-of-the-garden peas, especially when cooked with new potatoes. Peas belong to the legume family and provide lots of vitamin A, B, and C. Peas are a cool-season crop and do best planted early when the soil temperature reaches 45°F. Peas must also be supported off

☻ Peas are an early spring plant and a garden tradition in many areas of the country.

the ground to produce any kind of crop; even bush-type peas need some support.

Types. Peas are available in a number of varieties and three basic types: English or shelling peas, snap peas, and snow peas. Shell peas are the most common. You eat the pods and all on snap peas or wait until they mature and shell them. Snow peas, also called sugar or Chinese peas, are eaten whole when the peas first begin

to form in the pods. They're delicious raw, steamed, or their most popular use, stir-fried.

Culture

A. Propagation: direct seeded
B. Amount needed for 100-ft. row: 1 lb.
C. Where to plant: direct sun
D. When to plant: Plant in early spring, as early as two months before your last frost date. Can also be fall planted in some southern areas.
E. Row spacing: 24 in.
F. Plant spacing: 3 in.
G. Depth: 1 in.
H. How much per person: fresh, 10 to 15 ft.; processed, 20 to 30 ft.
I. Days from planting to eating stage: 50 to 60

⊗ Peas are available in three basic types: shelling, snap, or snow. The latter features edible pods.

Requirements

Soil type: Does best in rich, deep, and well drained because of the early-spring planting time. Peas do not do well in clay or hard-panned soil.

pH: 7

Fertilizer: Although peas fix nitrogen from the soil, they use most of it. Use a general-purpose fertilizer. Peas

❽ Peas need support of some type.

mulch the area for the pea rows in the fall. Merely rake back the mulch; dig a furrow in the soil, which will be more friable; and plant the seed. Peas require steady moisture and, as the weather gets warmer, protection for the roots from heat. When the plants appear, simply rake the mulch back in place. Peas can be planted in double rows for increased productivity.

Most peas need support in the way of some sort of trellis. A common trellis is three-foot poultry

❽ Peas and potatoes make a great early spring food crop.

do best without additional nitrogen, which may cause excessive foliage growth.

Growing tips. Peas are usually the first things seeded in the garden, often when the soil is still cold, wet, and clumpy from the winter. Since peas mature early, leaving space for successive planting of other vegetables, I plant peas along one side of the garden, tilling only that area and leaving the rest of the garden to till for later planting. Another tactic is to heavily netting fastened to wooden stakes. One method is to plant a row on either side of the trellis. For the best yields, peas need to be inoculated with nitrogen-fixing rhizobia. Seed sellers also sell the inoculant. During dry weather, keep the peas well watered but do not use overhead watering, as it may cause mildew. If you cultivate, do shallow cultivation to prevent root damage. In some areas of long spring weather, peas can be planted successively for a number of crops, but they do not do well in hot weather.

Pests. Peas are not bothered by many pests.

Harvest. Snap and shell peas should be harvested once the pods have filled. Early, immature peas are the most tender. For fuller, "meaty" peas, wait until the pods are solid.

Storage. Keep them stored in perforated plastic bags or containers in the refrigerator. Pressure can, freeze, or dehydrate the surplus.

***

Peppers

Description. Peppers are another all-time favorite food to grow. They're extremely versatile and can be grown in traditional garden rows, raised beds, and even in containers on a deck or patio. Peppers are a much favored food in many dishes, and they're good for you. One sweet green pepper has almost all the vitamin C you need for a day. A mature red or yellow pepper has even more.

Types. Peppers come in a wide range of varieties: sweet, hot, really hot, red, yellow, green, orange, and even purple.

Culture

A. Propagation: Peppers need warm weather and a long growing season. For this reason, most peppers

◉ Peppers are another popular homegrown food crop and are available in a wide range of varieties from hot to mild, red, green, and yellow.

are grown from indoor started seeds for transplants.

B. Amount needed for 100-ft. row: ½ oz.
C. Where to plant: direct sun
D. When to plant: late spring, after all chance of frost
E. Row spacing: 30 in.
F. Plant spacing: 18 in.
G. Depth: 2 to 3 in. for transplants
H. How much per person: fresh, 2 to 3 plants; processed, 3 to 6 plants
I. Days from planting to eating stage: 70 to 80

◉ Peppers do best grown with mulch and staked.

Requirements

Soil type: rich, well drained
pH: 6.5 to 7.0
Fertilizer: Use an all-purpose fertilizer. Overapplication of nitrogen can create excess foliage and a late-season bloom.

Growing tips. Pepper plants are extremely popular in the garden centers. Peppers are easy to grow as long as you have a hot summer. They also do best in high-humidity areas but will withstand drought fairly well. You can also start your own pepper plants indoors from eight to ten weeks before setting out. Not only does this save money, but it also gives you a bigger choice of varieties. It doesn't take a lot of pepper plants to feed a family. I normally start about half of the seeds in a packet, saving the rest for the following year. I don't get quite as good germination on the second year but still have plenty of seedlings. Mulching can help a great deal in holding moisture for the plants. I run a soaker hose along the pepper plants and cover it with mulch. The plants often grow four feet or taller, so I support them by tying them to wooden stakes with soft cloth strips. It pays to keep the peppers picked to keep them producing throughout the season.

Pests. Peppers have few pests.

Harvest. Harvest sweet peppers as soon as the peppers are big enough. They should be well formed and firm. Almost all sweet peppers, with the exception of yellow peppers, will turn red if left to mature fully. For hot peppers, pick what you need through the season for dishes but leave the majority on the plant. Pull the plant at the end of the season and hang in a warm place to dry. Under a porch roof is a good choice.

Storage. Store sweet peppers in the refrigerator for two to three weeks and freeze surplus. Sweet peppers can be roasted, peeled, and frozen or diced and dehydrated. Dried hot peppers can be left on the plant and hung in a basement or other area. Or you can pull off some hot peppers and string on thread for use in the kitchen as well as for decor. Excess green chili peppers should be frozen.

∗∗∗

Potato

Description. Until you grow your own potatoes, you won't realize the difference between store-bought and homegrown. The flavor and texture are greatly different. New potatoes are

☻ Potatoes are a traditional homegrown food. They do take up space but produce a lot of food.

a melt-in-your-mouth treat you definitely won't find at the market. It takes space to grow potatoes, but they grow fairly easily. Potatoes are a cool-season plant and must be planted early in the spring, right after the peas.

Types. Potatoes are available as reds or whites, depending on the skin color. And a fairly large variety is available in each color. Some varieties are best for mashed potatoes, some best for bakers, and some are good all-around potatoes.

Culture

A. Propagation: planting "eyes" or seed potatoes
B. Amount needed for 100-ft. row: 10 lbs.

C. Where to plant: direct sun

D. When to plant: early spring

E. Row spacing: 30 in.

F. Plant spacing: 12 in.

G. Depth: 4 in.

H. How much per person: 50 to 100 ft. fresh and stored

I. Days from planting to eating stage: 100 to 120

Requirements

Soil type: Because they're a root crop, potatoes do best in a deep, rich, friable soil.

pH: It ranges from 6.0 to 6.5, but do not overlime, as this can cause scabby potatoes.

Fertilizer: Use the general-purpose. Potatoes do best with applications of phosphorus and side-dressing with nitrogen once they bloom.

Growing tips. Potatoes are grown from pieces cut from seed potatoes or,

⊗ Potatoes are grown from chunks cut from seed potatoes. Each chunk must have two eyes.

in some instances, small whole-seed potatoes. These are not the same potatoes sold in the supermarket as eating potatoes. Seed potatoes are treated to help prevent rotting until they sprout. My dad used to keep the smallest of his potato crop to plant the next year's crop, but I've found this reduces production somewhat. Seed potatoes are normally available locally and usually the varieties that do best in your area. Seed potatoes are also available mail

⊗ Potatoes are most commonly grown in rows.

order with a great selection of varieties. Make sure you use certified disease-free seed potatoes.

If planting chunks, cut seed potatoes into chunks about 1½ × 1½ inches and with at least one eye. I prefer two eyes. Allow the cut chunks to dry for a day or two in a shady, cool spot. Traditionally, potatoes are planted in rows. Apply a layer of well-rotted manure and a general fertilizer with high phosphorus. Till manure and fertilizer deeply into the soil and then dig a four- to six-inch-deep furrow. Plant the cut side down, spacing the chunks twelve to sixteen inches apart. Pull the soil up and over the chunks, covering them well to prevent

frostbite and rotting. When the plants sprout and begin to grow, continue to pull soil up around the row on both sides. Pick off the blossoms as they appear to keep the energy in producing the spuds.

In years past, I've discovered a heavy hay or straw mulch to be the easy-does-it method. I continue to add mulch as the plants grow. When it comes time to dig potatoes, there's no digging involved. Simply pull back the mulch and pull out the potatoes. Potatoes shouldn't be grown in the same place each year, so I alternate with another cool-season crop—peas. You don't, however, need to have a long row of potatoes to enjoy homegrown.

Potatoes can also be grown in a number of imaginative ways. I've grown them in old tires, placing one

⊗ Potatoes can also be grown in old automobile tires, or with a potato tower of wire and plastic.

⊗ First dig a furrow.

⊗ The cut chunks are then placed in the furrow.

⊗ Then the chunks are fully covered.

tire in place, adding some soil, planting the chunks, and then adding more soil and tires to create a minipotato patch. If you don't like the looks or having to deal with old tires, a better tactic is to create a cage of hog or chicken wire, line the inside with black plastic, and plant like the tires, starting seed potatoes and adding soil as the plants grow.

Pests. The Colorado potato beetle can be a major pest. This is one place I use Sevin dust to prevent an infestation.

Harvest. Harvest new potatoes as soon as the blossoms appear. If you're using straw mulch, simply reach under the straw and "steal" a few small potatoes. Wait until the plants die down to harvest mature potatoes. Do not leave potatoes in the ground and exposed to the sun after the tops die down, as the potatoes will turn green and become useless. Wash dirt from the potatoes and allow them to cure in a shady, well-ventilated place, but out of the light.

⊗ Potatoes can be stored in a basement or cellar but must be kept away from sources of light.

Storage. Store in a cool place with fairly high humidity, good ventilation, and no light.

***

Pumpkin

Description. Halloween wouldn't be Halloween without jack-o'-lanterns, and Thanksgiving wouldn't be Thanksgiving without pumpkin pies. Pumpkins are fun and fairly easy to grow. They're also a great way to introduce youngsters to growing their own fun food. Pumpkins are very good for you, and that includes the roasted seeds.

Types. Pumpkins are available in a number of varieties and in a wide range of sizes, from the tiny decorative pumpkins to the giants grown for big pumpkin contests. In between are numerous varieties for cooking. The latter tend to have a sweet taste, are smaller, and more tender than larger varieties.

Culture

A. Propagation: direct seeded
B. Amount needed for 100-ft. row: 1 oz.
C. Where to plant: sun to partial shade
D. When to plant: after danger of frost
E. Row spacing: 48 in.
F. Plant spacing: 60 in.
G. Depth: ½ in.
H. How much per person per year: 3 to 5 hills
I. Days from planting to eating stage: 110

Requirements

Soil type: rich, deep

pH: 6.5 to 7.0

Fertilizer: general-purpose at time of planting

Growing tips. A traditional method of planting pumpkins is in the corn patch. Pumpkins don't like extremely hot or cold weather, and the corn provides partial shade. Plant about a dozen seeds in each hill. After the plants are well established and all danger from bugs is past, thin to three plants per hill. Adding compost or well-rotted manure to the hills at planting will give pumpkins a boost. If you want to grow giant pumpkins, pick off all but one or two blossoms at the beginning of their growth.

Pests. Pumpkins have much the same problem as squash with squash beetles, Colorado potato bugs, and many others.

Harvest. Harvest when the skin darkens and turns hard. They must be harvested before frost.

Storage. Store in a cool, dry place.

***

Radish

Description. Radishes are another fun crop almost anyone can grow almost anywhere. The only exception is extremely hot weather. Radishes tend to turn to seed production in hot weather. They're basically a cool- to cold-weather crop. Radishes can be grown throughout the winter in some areas, and almost anywhere it's cold in hotbeds or cold frames. Radishes can be planted spring or fall for a fall or winter crop.

Types. Although many know radishes only as the bright red globes sold in the supermarkets, radishes are available in a wide range of varieties, from tiny to big winter radishes, and in a wide array of colors.

Culture

A. Propagation: direct seeded
B. Amount needed for 100-ft. row: 1 oz.
C. Where to plant: direct sun
D. When to plant: very early spring, late fall
E. Row spacing: 18 in.
F. Plant spacing: 1 in.
G. Depth: ¼ in.

H. How much per person per year: 5 to 10 ft.
I. Days from planting to eating stage: 25 to 35

Requirements

Soil type: Will grow just about anywhere but does best in a deep, rich soil.

pH: 6.5

Fertilizer: general-purpose at planting

Growing tips. Because they're so easy to grow, radishes are a great kid's "grow your own." Make successive plantings to provide salad fixings from midspring through early summer. Keep watered and grow fast. Slow-growing radishes have a pungent flavor and woody texture. Interplant radishes with any number of slower-germinating seeds in the

❷ Radishes are another fun crop that brightens summer salads.

spring to mark rows. Pull radishes as they mature, creating a natural thinning of the secondary plants.

Pests. It has few pests.

Harvest. Harvest when half to one inch in diameter for globe radishes.

Storage. Wash well and store in perforated plastic bags in the refrigerator. Winter radishes can be stored the same as for carrots.

***

Spinach

Description. Popeye, the famous cartoon character, had it right. Spinach is the super food. Full of vitamins, minerals, and cancer-fighting compounds, spinach can be served raw or cooked. Spinach is a cool-season

❷ Spinach is a super food — super good for you — and easy to grow.

vegetable. It will not do well in either hot or cold weather.

Types. Spinach comes in several varieties, with some, such as Asian types, more tolerant of harsh weather. New Zealand spinach is more heat resistant.

Culture

A. Propagation: direct seeded but may also be transplanted
B. Amount needed for 100-ft. row: 1 oz.
C. Where to plant: direct sun
D. When to plant: early spring, midfall
E. Row spacing: 18 in.
F. Plant spacing: 3 in.
G. Depth: ¼ in.
H. How much per person per year: fresh, 5 to 10 ft.; processed, 10 to 15 ft.
I. Days from planting to eating stage: 40 to 50

⊗ Salad greens, such as spinach or lettuce, can be pulled as plants.

⊗ You may also use garden shears to cut off the tops.

Requirements

Soil type: deep, rich, well-drained soil

pH: 6.5

Fertilizer: high nitrogen

Growing tips. Spinach is easy to grow under the right weather conditions. This is a great plant for raised-bed gardening. Make successive plantings two weeks apart for a continuous supply through the spring and early summer months. Then plant again in the fall and use row covers to provide a crop through early winter.

Pests. It has few pests, but beetles can be a problem.

Harvest. Harvest leaves when they reach a suitable size. Pinch off outer leaves and tops to keep the plant producing. Or harvest the whole plant.

Storage. It doesn't store well. Keep in a damp cloth in the refrigerator or blanch and freeze excess.

***

Squash

Description. Squash is one of America's original foods. Squash grows easily and often, as in the case of zucchini which produces so much so fast, it's hard to find something to do with all the harvest. Squash is extremely good for you, with winter squash providing lots of vitamin A. The deep orange flesh of winter squash also has a lot of beta-carotene, a cancer-fighting compound.

Types. Squash is available as both a summer and winter variety.

◈ Squash is an all-American native food.

◈ Squash is available in both summer and winter varieties. This is a yellow zucchini.

◈ This is a summer squash.

Two types are available; bush varieties are planted in hills four to five feet apart, sprawling vine types require eight or more feet of room between plants. Squash is also a very decorative plant with lots of unusual colors and shapes, including acorn, butternut, and even vegetable spaghetti.

Culture

A. Propagation: direct seeded or transplanted
B. Amount needed for 100-ft. row: summer, 1 oz.; winter, ½ oz.
C. Where to plant: direct sun
D. When to plant: summer, late spring, winter
E. Row spacing: summer, 48 in.; winter, 60 in.
F. Plant spacing: summer, 48 in.; winter, 60 in.
G. Depth: ½ in.
H. How much per person per year: summer, 2 to 4 hills; winter, 4 to 5 hills
I. Days from planting to eating stage: summer, 80 to 90; winter, 125 to 160

Requirements

Soil type: rich, well drained, some sand, no clay
pH: 6.5
Fertilizer: Use general-purpose and side-dress with fertilizer low in nitrogen. Excess nitrogen causes excessive growth of vines, with less fruit.

Growing tips. Squash should be planted after all danger of frost. If you want earlier plants, start indoors in peat or newspaper pots. The plants do not do well if their roots are disturbed during transplanting. Plant in hills, adding compost and dried manure in a hole dug for each hill. Cover with a bit of topsoil and plant seeds or transplant. If direct seeding, plant about six seeds to a hill. You can grow the bush varieties in raised beds, and they do quite well. Space them about one and a half to two feet apart for intensive growing. Mulch and keep well watered. Since summer squash produces so heavily, you won't need a lot of plants. But plant more winter squash as winter keepers. Keep well watered and mulched.

Pests. Squash have quite a few pests, most notably squash bugs, squash borers, and a number of beetles. Regularly dusting Sevin or with wood ashes can help keep down infestations.

Harvest. Pick summer squash while they are still young and tender. Pick every day or so during their growing season, as they grow fast. Pick winter squash when the skins can't be pierced with your fingernail.

Storage. Keep summer squash in the refrigerator for a short time.

⊗ Sweet potatoes are extremely versatile and easy to grow. They can also be extremely productive.

Freeze for future use. Store winter squash in a warm, dry place, such as a basement, in a single layer on a shelf so they have good air circulation.

***

Sweet Potatoes

Description. Basically a tropical plant, sweet potatoes do well in the south, but anyone with one hundred days of frost-free growing can grow sweet potatoes. Sweet potatoes are an extremely versatile food. They can be baked, deep-fried, made into casseroles and even pies. They also provide lots of health benefits. One sweet potato can provide all the carotene and vitamin A, plus about a third of the daily requirement of vitamin C. Sweet potatoes are fairly easy to grow and can be stored through the winter months. Nothing can be easier to prepare—merely microwave a few minutes and add a dollop of butter.

Types. A handful of varieties are available, mostly depending on days to harvest. Growers in the north should use the shorter-season varieties. Sweet potatoes are available with different skin colors, but taste is similar.

⊗ Sweet potatoes are planted as slips. They should be planted in raised furrows.

Culture

A. Propagation: by rooted slips

B. Amount needed for 100-ft. row: 100 slips

C. Where to plant: direct sun

D. When to plant: after all danger of frost

E. Row spacing: 30 in.

F. Plant spacing: 12 in.

G. Depth: 2 in.

H. How much per person per year: 2 to 6 plants

I. Days from planting to eating stage: 90 to 150

Requirements

Soil type: deep, rich sandy loam
pH: 6

Fertilizer: lots of well-rotted manure, general-purpose

Growing tips. Sweet potato slips are available mail order and usually through local garden centers. You can also very easily start your own with purchased potatoes. But you may not know the variety. Slips can be started in two ways. One simple method is to place the sweet potato in a glass or jar of water.

Stick toothpicks into the potato around the center, then suspend in

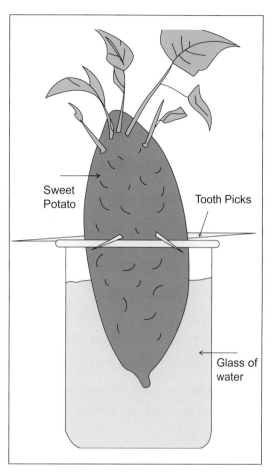

⮑ You can start your own slips by placing a tuber in a jar of water.

the water with the tiny purple eye, or end facing away from the root end up. Sprouts should appear in a few weeks. The more common method for producing large numbers of slips is to place a little seed-starting soil or coarse sand in a container, such as a seed flat. Place a layer of sweet potatoes on the material, cover and water well. Provide bottom heat and a little

⊗ You can also start from tubers placed horizontally in starting flats of sand.

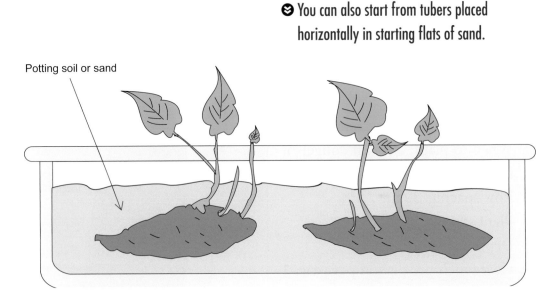

Potting soil or sand

light, for instance from a grow light. Sprouts should appear in from three to five weeks. Keep the slips in good light, warm, and well watered until time to plant.

When you're ready to plant, simply grasp a slip and yank it off. You won't hurt it. Sweet potatoes are normally planted in ridges six to eighteen inches high. Create these ridges by layering compost, coarse sand, well-rotted manure and then mixing then well. These ridges heat quicker than level ground. Make rows about thirty inches apart and space the plants about eighteen inches apart. Dig holes for the transplants or slips, water the hole, and plant the slip, making sure the soil is well packed around the slip.

Keep well watered and in a few weeks the vines will start to sprawl. Mulching around the plant and between the rows cuts down on weeding and keeps moisture in the soil. Sweet potatoes can be grown even easier, especially in the northern areas with black plastic. Prepare the ridge as before and create a furrow down the center of the top. Cover the entire area with black plastic at least two weeks before planting. This will warm up the soil. Wait until late afternoon of the day you intend to plant and then cut small slits in the plastic over the row and spaced about eighteen inches apart. Dig holes for the slips, add water, and transplant. Make sure to firm the soil well up around the plants and the plastic doesn't cover any leaves. In the south, remove the black plastic after the plants are well established and mulch heavily. I simply fold the plastic down off the ridges but leave on both sides and then add a heavy layer of hay mulch. Keep well watered and stand back. Sweet potato vines can really cover an area.

Pests. Sweet potatoes are bothered by few pests. Underground critters, mice, and field rats really like to chew on the delicious tubers.

Harvest. Harvest in the fall before frosts. Use a potato fork and be careful in digging not to damage the tender roots. Cure for a week in a warm place (80° to 85°F is ideal) but out of the sun.

Storage. Store at 55° to 60°F with a fairly high humidity. If in a basement near a furnace, place in ventilated boxes or on shelves and keep covered with burlap sacks, periodically moistened.

***

Tomatoes

Description. The favorite home-grown food is tomatoes. Almost everyone who grows food grows tomatoes, even patio gardeners who

❂ Tomatoes are available in a wide range of varieties, including these tiny "grape" tomatoes.

❂ Tomatoes are the all-time favorite food to grow.

simply like the decor of a tomato plant. Homegrown tomatoes also have a flavor and texture that is nothing like the supermarket tomatoes. Tomatoes are also very easy and fun to grow and provide lots of health benefits; they are an excellent source of vitamins A and C as well as lycopene, a compound that researchers believe that could help prevent prostate cancer in men. Tomatoes are also extremely versatile. They can be eaten fresh, whole, in salads and are a main ingredient in many meals. And they're great canned as juice and in a number of sauces.

Types. Tomatoes are available in numerous varieties, including tiny, huge, red, yellow, black, all purpose, and orange-striped. Most local garden centers carry tomatoes favored in their area. The larger box stores carry standard varieties. Mail-order seed companies produce a very wide range of tomatoes, both as plants and seeds. Tomatoes are available in two types: determinate and indeterminate. Determinate tomatoes ripen over three to four weeks and are on bushier vines. Indeterminate tomatoes will continue to grow and produce tomatoes all season long or until frost. Tomatoes are susceptible to a number of diseases and pests; however, many varieties have been bred to withstand diseases. Tomato plant or seed sellers use letters to denote resistance. *V* stands for verticillium wilt disease, *FF* stands for resistance to fusarium wilt race I and II, *N* for root-knot nematodes (a soil-dwelling pest common in the south), and *T* for tobacco mosaic virus.

⊗ Tomatoes are most commonly started by setting out transplants.

Culture

A. Propagation: can be direct seeded but more commonly transplanted
B. Amount needed for 100-ft. row: .125 oz.

Growing tips. There are probably as many different ways to grow tomatoes as there are varieties. After over fifty years of growing tomatoes, I've probably tried them all and settled on a system that works for me. I start my own seed indoors. The tomatoes are grown in big cages, about twenty-four inches in diameter, made of welded concrete reinforcing wire. A week or so before time to plant, I lay a soaker hose down the length of the garden and position my tomato row. I lay the cages near the soaker hose as "spacers." Using a shovel, dig a hole on both sides of the soaker hose. The hole will be about a foot deep. A bit of compost or well-rotted manure is shoveled into the hole and worked into the soil. You don't want too rich a soil, so go lightly on the manure. When it comes time to transplant, I wait until

❷ You can start your own transplants from seed.

C. Where to plant: direct sun
D. When to plant: after all danger of frost
E. Row spacing: 48 in.
F. Plant spacing: 18 in. (staked or cages)
G. Depth: 2 in.
H. How much per person per year: fresh, 3 to 6 plants; processed, 6 to 12 plants
I. Days from planting to eating stage: 75 to 90

Requirements

Soil type: Tomatoes don't need an overly rich soil.

pH: 6.5 to 7.0

Fertilizer: Too much nitrogen can cause heavy foliage with less fruit. Applications of phosphorus and potassium can help.

❷ My favorite method of growing tomato plants is in large metal mesh cages, with mulch and a soaker hose for water.

⊗ Using this method I can grow a lot of tomatoes in a small space.

late afternoon, position the plants near the holes, and mark the variety locations in a notebook. A teaspoon of Epsom salts is applied to each hole, and the holes are well watered.

The plants are removed from the pots, and the bottom leaves pinched off. The plants are laid in the holes with their root ends facing outward or away from the center. The stems are gently bent so only the tops of the transplants are above soil level. The soil shoveled out is raked back and firmed over the transplanted stems and roots. Then the plants are watered again. After the plants have become established and before the weeds start growing, mulch

heavily around the plants and over the soaker hose. Then the cages are positioned over the plants, two plants to a cage.

Because of high winds in our area, I drive stakes every third cage and tie cages to each other and to the stakes. Other than regular watering, that's all I do until blossoms appear. Then I begin to add a liquid tomato fertilizer or one high in phosphorus. You will also need to apply some nitrogen once the plants start to set fruit. Nitrogen applied too early or too much can cause the plants to give all their

⊗ Properly setting out the transplants is important.

energy to producing foliage instead of fruits. Blossom-end rot is a common tomato problem, usually caused by inconsistent watering. Tomatoes require lots of water; however, don't water overhead, as this can cause problems with mildew. Many tomato growers pinch off the sucker stems that grow between the main and secondary stem. I don't bother with this, as I've found it doesn't increase production that much.

Pests. Tomatoes have pests, principally the horned worm, Colorado potato beetles, and even grasshoppers. The latter can really work over the plants in dry weather when other surrounding foliage is dry and dead.

Harvest. Although many suggest harvesting when the fruit is bright red or ripe, I prefer to harvest red tomatoes when they first begin their blush of color. Tomatoes will ripen just as easily off the vine if placed in a shady, warm area. This method keeps the plants producing heavily. Pick all the green tomatoes just before the first frost. Some can be used in green tomato dishes, but most are left to ripen. I usually pick the first week of October and have ripe tomatoes for Thanksgiving.

Storage. Tomatoes can be kept in the refrigerator, a cool place, canned, or frozen.

***

⊗ Set the plants horizontally for best results.

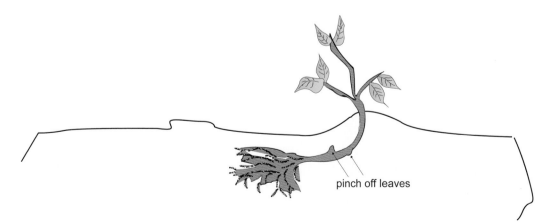

pinch off leaves

Turnip

Description. Turnips and their relative, rutabagas, are an extremely important food, grown not only for human consumption but also as a livestock food crop. Turnips are extremely easy to grow. They are a cool-season crop and can be grown in spring or fall, but more commonly in the fall.

Types. Not a lot of varieties are available, but turnip seed is available locally at almost any garden supply or farm store.

Culture

A. Propagation: direct seeded
B. Amount needed for 100-ft. row: ½ oz.
C. Where to plant: direct sun
D. When to plant: mid- to late summer
E. Row spacing: 18 in.
F. Plant spacing: 6 in.
G. Depth: ¼ in.
H. How much per person per year: 10 to 15 ft.
I. Days from planting to eating stage: 35 to 60

Requirements

Soil type: good, loose, friable soil
pH: 6.5 to 7.0
Fertilizer: general-purpose

Growing tips. Turnips have few growing requirements except for cool weather and a relatively good soil. The soil should be fairly loose and friable for the roots to grow properly. Do not sow too many seeds, as crowded plants produce less. Keep well watered.

Pests. Root maggots and flea beetles can be a problem.

Harvest. Can be harvested any time they're one inch or bigger. Turnips become sweeter after frosts and can withstand several light freezes.

Storage. Store in a cool, moist area such as a root cellar. Or cover with heavy layers of straw and leave in the garden.

***

Watermelon

Description. For many folks, summer wouldn't be summer without watermelon. Once you taste the sweetness of homegrown watermelons out of your own garden, you'll definitely be spoiled. Watermelons are very easy to grow, but they require a long hot growing season, and the sprawling vines take a lot of space.

Types. A number of varieties are available, including honeydew melons, grown in the same manner as traditional watermelons, with red to yellow flesh, white or green flesh. Melons are available in numerous sizes, from giants to "personal" size. Watermelons are available seeded or seedless. The seeded are the easiest to grow. Seedless seeds come with pollinator seeds that must also be planted.

Culture

A. Propagation: direct seeded or started indoors in peat or paper pots

B. Amount needed for 100-ft. row: 1 oz.

⊗ Growing watermelons takes a lot of space and effort, but it's a very healthful summertime treat you can grow yourself.

⊗ Growing in black plastic can make the chore easier.

C. Where to plant: direct sun

D. When to plant: after last frost

E. Row spacing: 96 in.

F. Plant spacing: 96 in.

G. Depth: ½ in.

H. How much per person per year: 3 to 6 hills

I. Days from planting to eating stage: 65 to 95

Requirements

Soil type: deep, rich sandy loam

pH: 6.5 to 7.0

Fertilizer: general-purpose

Growing tips. Watermelons are grown in hills. If your soil doesn't have sand, add a bit of coarse sand, as well as lots of well-rotted manure to the location of the hills. I couldn't grow watermelons until I started growing them on black plastic. This not only warms up the soil for an earlier start, but you also don't have to weed around the sprawling vines. Watermelon vines don't like to be disturbed. I place a perforated plastic container in each hill and plant eight seeds or three transplants. The seeds are thinned to three or four plants after the seedlings are well started. I also drive a wooden stake in the location of each hill because once the vines really get going, you won't know the location of the roots. Keep the roots watered and use a liquid spray fertilizer.

Pests. Watermelons have few pests, but Colorado potato bugs, squash bugs, and some beetles can be a problem.

Harvest. Forget about thumping the melon. After a number of years growing, I still can't determine a ripe melon by this method. The rind should be dull, not shiny, and a whitish to yellow spot should be on the underside. Most importantly, if the tiny curling tendril nearest the stem of the melon is dried, the melon is ripe.

Storage. In your tummy. Watermelon will store at room temperature for about a week. Or it can be kept in a refrigerator or cooler for two to three weeks at 45° to 60°F.

7

Growing Food for Fall and Winter

When most folks think of growing food, they think of the spring and summer growing seasons, but some foods can be grown in the fall as well. With the right circumstances and a little work, some foods can be grown year-round. I'll have to admit to being a bit lax in winter gardening. Usually I'm worn-out from gardening and putting up food about the time I'm supposed to be starting a fall and winter garden. On the other hand, growing food in the fall can actually be easier in many ways than in the spring and summer. This is especially so of the cool-season crops such as cabbage, spinach, turnips, and others. The pests of summer, heat, and weeds are not as much a problem in late-season gardening. Growing

« You can grow some foods in fall and winter with a few tricks. Cabbage is an easy fall and winter food crop.

fall and winter foods can be done in four ways: in the garden unprotected, in the garden protected, taken inside at the start of cold weather, or grown completely inside a greenhouse, sunroom, or even next to a sunny door or window.

Growing in the Garden

Some foods are easier to grow in the fall than others, and cool season crops are the easiest. Not only do they grow best in cool weather, but they also typically have a fairly short growing season. If you plan to grow these crops unprotected, the first step is to determine the timing of your average first fall frost. The plants you grow and the timing of their planting depends

❷ One method is to grow plants in a wire cage.

on that factor. In most instances, you should sow seeds, or set plants, about six to seven weeks before your first fall frost. This will vary somewhat, depending on your climate, late-summer/fall temperature, and available moisture as well as time to maturity. Frost doesn't hurt some plants, for instance, turnips and Brussels sprouts.

If direct seeding, prepare the soil in the same manner as for a spring food crop. If the weather is hot and dry, you may wish to water the soil well before seeding. Plants that do well direct seeded include the following: carrots, turnips, lettuce, spinach, and radishes. Broccoli and cabbage can be direct seeded, but I prefer to start seeds in flats in a shady place, but with good, but not direct sun, such as under an awning or porch. I also start some lettuce and spinach to get a "jump" on the fall garden. Transplant in the garden after about four to six weeks when the plants are well started and usually just about the first of the cool weather in our part of the country. I typically start seeds in early August to set out in late September.

Most of these plants will do well even through light frosts without any protection, but you can greatly extend

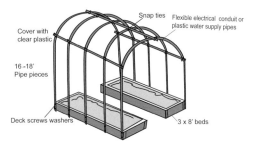

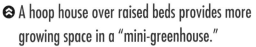

⊗ A hoop house over raised beds provides more growing space in a "mini-greenhouse."

⊗ Use plastic to cover the cages in extreme cold weather.

the season by adding protection. The simplest plant protection is to cover the plants the evening before a nightly frost with a light blanket or tarp. Floating row covers are a better method.

⊗ Radishes and lettuce are also good choices for a covered fall bed.

These are available as lightweight, clear plastic coverings from seed and nursery supply companies. The covers are simply spread or floated over the plants and will increase soil and air temperature, trapping heat during the day and releasing it at night to keep plants growing even in cold weather. The TunLcover from Burpee is an even better choice. These expand to eighteen feet long and are placed over the row to act like a minigreenhouse. The TunLcover will keep temperatures up to 25°F warmer than the air temperature. With these you can grow through the fall frosts and right through the winter with some plants in some areas.

All fall-planted foods do well in raised beds; in fact, that's the easiest method of growing them. Here's where you can really get creative with protecting fall and winter plants. I build raised-bed cages from welded concrete reinforcing wire to fit over my raised beds and protect the plants from deer and other critters during the spring and summer seasons. It's easy in fall and winter to simply add a clear plastic cover over these cages and grow through frost and freezing weather, lifting the clear plastic as needed during extrawarm, sunny days.

The next step up is the hoop house. These can be built over rows or larger raised beds, and you can actually get inside them to work. They're basically instant greenhouses and consist of plastic plumbing pipe bent into hoops and covered with clear plastic. The edges are held down with hay bales or other means. Hoop houses do have some problems in windy areas.

Cold Frames and Hotbeds

Another great way of growing through the fall and winter months as well as having a great place to harden off spring plants is in cold frames and hotbeds. Cold frames are basically raised beds with lids that allow sunlight to filter in and heat the interior,

◎ A cold frame or hot bed extends food growing through both fall and winter and is great for early-season spring planting.

but keep out the cold. They can be purchased or very easily homemade. Cold frames can be constructed as permanent free-standing structures, as attachments to the south side of a building, or even as portable units if bolts are used in the corners so they can easily be disassembled and moved or stored as desired. If you construct several raised beds early in the spring and use them through the summer months, you might simply add a cold frame lid to one in the fall for winter gardening.

The main difference between a cold frame and a raised bed is that the bed surface in a cold frame must be low enough to allow for plants, such as lettuce, to grow unhindered. This usually means a depth of six to eight inches.

A discarded old wooden storm window or even recycled window sashes can be used as the lid, or you can create your own using double-strength glass or special greenhouse fiberglass panels. The latter are safer, as they are not prone to breakage. Construction of the cold frame box is the same as for raised beds of treated lumber. The box for the cold frame, however, should be set in the ground to prevent cold air from seeping in around the edges. Or mound soil up around the edges of the box.

A cold frame works best if it has a slanted top to allow more of the sun's rays to reach the interior of the box, compensating for winter's fewer daylight hours. Although the lid can be left unattached, it is more efficient if the lid is secured to the back of the box with butt hinges. A prop board or a stick is used to hold the lid partially open to allow air circulation. During warm winter days, the lid is propped open to cool and closed in the late afternoon to keep in the heat during the night. It's a good idea to include an outdoor thermometer in the cold

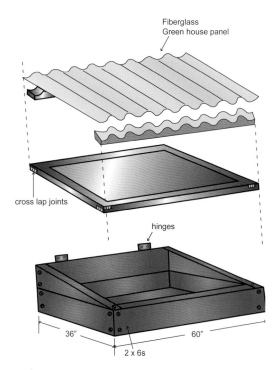

❂ You can build a cold frame or hot bed quite easily.

frame to better monitor and maintain temperatures.

The old-fashioned hotbed was a major feature on many farmsteads of the past. The hotbed is actually nothing more than a cold frame with heat supplied. In the olden days, horse manure, a very hot manure, was dug well below the planting soil to provide the heat. These days special electric heating cables do the job much easier and with less hassle and smell. If using a heating cable, remove the soil below the bottom edge of the frame and put a two-inch layer of sand in place. Lay the cable over the sand and then add the soil on top. (Make sure the heating cable specifies it is for use as a buried cable.)

Another method in extending the season is to simply drag plants indoors. If you're already container gardening, this is a no-brainer. A sunroom is the ideal, but a sunny window or patio door can also provide a food-growing space. It's important to check frequently and keep indoor winter-grown plants well watered and lightly fertilized with a water-soluble fertilizer.

The last and ultimate winter-growing space is a greenhouse. Serious food growers dream of their own greenhouse, and yes, you can grow just about anything in a greenhouse. This, however, is labor intensive. It takes daily work to maintain the temperature and humidity of a greenhouse for winter growing. Not to mention the daily care of the plants. Home greenhouses can be as large and expensive as you can imagine and just as simple and economical. Our first greenhouse was simply a 6 × 12 foot A-frame nailed together and covered with clear plastic. The plastic lasted through one season; the greenhouse recovered twice through three seasons. But we grew a lot of food for our growing family. Then came a fancy all-glass greenhouse on the side of our house. We used it for a number of years, but it faced the road and driveway entrance and when not in use during the off season was an eyesore. Finally we built the greenhouse we have today. It's basically a very small 6 × 8 foot and attached to the south side of a garden storage shed. It has a concrete floor, fiberglass panels, and is passively heated. The heat comes from black plastic barrels filled with water along the back of the greenhouse. There is no electricity or other heat source. Even when temperatures get below 10°F, it stays well above freezing, usually around 40° to 42°F in those cold temperatures. This is true as long as the days are sunny.

8

Growing Perennial Foods

A number of plants are grown as perennials. Some annuals can, in fact, be grown as perennials in warm-season areas. True perennials, however, will continue to produce crops for many years if properly cared for. The most common perennials include the following: artichokes, asparagus, rhubarb, and horseradish.

Artichokes

First to distinguish is that the artichokes commonly found in grocery stores are globe artichokes, not Jerusalem artichokes, which are annuals. Not everyone can grow globe artichokes, no matter how much they might

❮ Some plants, such as rhubarb, are grown as perennials.

weeks before the last frost. Transplant after frost danger in rows six feet apart and with plants spaced three to four feet apart. Plant in a rich, well-fertilized soil. Planting in partial shade can help productivity in hot southern areas. The key to successfully growing artichokes is to keep a continuous supply of moisture and general-purpose fertilizer or plant food. Mulching the plants helps a great deal.

Asparagus

Asparagus is an old-time favorite that can produce lots of nutritious food for many years once it's started. It does, however, take some time and effort to get a bed started. Asparagus

desire this unusual and expensive gourmet food. Globe artichokes have very specific climate requirements. They are basically a Mediterranean plant and do best in areas with a long growing season, mild winters, and a damp climate. In southern areas with hot, dry climates, the globes become tough. You can grow globe artichokes in northern climates by growing them as annuals, digging up the plants and storing them over the winter in a cool, dark place.

Artichokes are commonly sold as seeds. Sow seeds indoors about eight

⊗ Asparagus is a traditional perennial favorite. Once started it will grow for years, producing a gourmet delight.

is a cool-season crop, and one of the most delicious of the spring vegetables. It is traditionally commercially grown in rows and in beds in gardens. Asparagus can be grown in a ground level or raised bed.

The latter offers a couple of advantages. It's easier to weed, and you can do a better job of soil preparation. The plants, however, may eventually spread outside the bed. The single most important facet in productively growing asparagus is ground preparation.

The bed must be very deep and rich. For the best results, you must dig the soil down eighteen to twenty-four inches deep. In hard-pan or rocky and clay areas, this may be almost impossible, and again, a raised bed may be the best choice. A slightly sandy soil that can maintain some moisture is the best.

Spade or dig the bed into a trench, setting the topsoil aside, near the trench. Fill the bottom six inches or so with compost and well-rotted manure. Add a six-inch or so layer of good garden soil, mixed well with a general-purpose organic fertilizer.

Asparagus is grown from crowns. Set the crowns on top of the soil in the trench, spaced twelve to eighteen

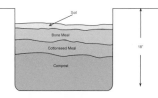

⊗ It's important to properly prepare and plant an asparagus bed.

⊗ Harvest when the spears are 6 to 10 inches high.

inches apart. Cover with a couple of inches of soil, compress the soil around the roots, and water well. Keep the plants well watered, and as they grow, continue to fill in the trench around the plants with good garden soil and compost. The trench should be completely filled in and slightly raised by the end of the first growing season.

Do not cut or pick any spears on the first growing season. Harvest the spears sparingly on the second year after planting. By the third season, you can expect to harvest a full crop. After harvest, apply a fertilizer of three to five pounds of general-purpose (10-10-10) or organic fertilizer per one hundred square feet. After the second season, remove the tops of the plants in late fall to prevent insects and diseases from wintering over. Several inches of a good mulch is important in cold climate areas to prevent winter damage to the crowns. Repeat the fertilizer application in the spring. Rake off the mulch, apply the fertilizer, and lightly rake into the soil surface.

To harvest, pick the spears when they are six to ten inches high and only for about six to eight weeks. Stop harvest after July 1 to allow the roots to store food for the coming year. Asparagus is great fresh but can also be frozen for future use.

Rhubarb

Another all-time favorite perennial is rhubarb. Rhubarb is also great for you with lots of vitamin C, potassium, and fiber. It, too, can be a challenge to grow in some areas. It does not do well in warm climates. Those in the south may have problems growing rhubarb consistently, although some varieties are bred for a better chance in warmer

❷ Rhubarb is a great health food and delicious in pies, cakes, and jams. It does best in areas with cool, moist summers but can be successfully grown in many other locales.

areas. Rhubarb grows best in areas with a cool, moist summer yet with cold winters that will freeze the ground fairly deep. Rhubarb grows as a perennial in these areas, as it requires winter dormancy.

If you live in a hot area, you'll need to grow a fresh crop each year. As you can guess, the state of Washington is the rhubarb capital of North America. The efforts are well worth it when you taste a rhubarb pie from your own garden. On the other hand, rhubarb is relatively easy to grow if conditions are right. Rhubarb can be grown from seed or from crowns. In most instances, you'll receive crowns from a mail-order or garden supply center. Rhubarb can be planted in the spring or fall, but spring is the most common planting time.

Like asparagus, rhubarb is a very heavy feeder, requiring a very rich soil. Grown properly, rhubarb is also a prolific spreader. The plants should be spaced three to four feet apart. Dig a hole at least twenty-four inches deep and twenty-four inches wide or about the size of a bushel basket. Fill the hole about two-thirds full with a mixture of half compost and half well-rotted manure.

Position the crowns on this layer and cover the crowns with a two-inch layer of compost with well-rotted manure mixed in. Compress down well and leave the crowns about three to four inches below the surface.

Rhubarb requires a deep, fertile soil. Dig a deep hole and add some bone meal.

Add some blood meal.

❷ Water well.

❷ Rhubarb comes as a crown or potted. Place in the fertilized, watered hole.

Water well and cover with a deep layer of mulch, leaving an open space around the crowns so they can grow up through the soil and mulch. Water and feed well throughout the growing season. Do not harvest the first season. Harvest lightly the second season.

By the third season, the plants should be well established, and you can harvest from early spring through early summer. In some areas, you may also have a fall harvest. If you don't harvest for a period of time, the stalks can become woody. Cut off all top growth, water well, and you'll often be rewarded with a second crop. During fall, cover with a layer of well-dried cow manure. In early spring, apply another layer of well-rotted cow manure or a general-purpose fertilizer.

❷ Fill in around the plant and compress the soil well then water again.

To harvest, cut off the stalks as they become about the diameter of your thumb or slightly larger. Remove the leaves. Do not eat the leaves, as they are poisonous.

About every six or seven years, like most perennials, you'll have to dig up the plants and divide them. When you notice the crown getting bigger and the stalks smaller, it's time to divide. Divide in fall or spring, but the best time is in early spring before the new stalks appear. Using a spade, dig around the crown about eight to ten inches deep, cutting the crown from the extending roots. Using a sharp, heavy knife, divide the crown following the natural indentations. The crown should be cut into pieces about the size of your fist, with at least one growing bud on each. Leave about a third of the original crown in place and set out the new crowns in another area.

Horseradish

Another popular perennial is horse-radish. Horseradish is a favorite condiment in a number of gourmet sauces and dishes. It is also one of the easiest plants to grow, and it doesn't take a lot of horseradish to feed a family. Plant horseradish in an out-of-the-way place in your garden because it can, in fact, spread quite rapidly. Like rhubarb, horseradish does best in cool climates and with deep, rich, moist soils. Horseradish is established from root cuttings or sets.

Dig holes about 12 × 12 inches and 8 to 10 inches apart in sun or partial shade. In hot climates, grow in partial shade. Growing in a raised bed allows you to contain the plant somewhat. Partially fill with compost and well-rotted manure. Set the root cuttings with the large end facing upward and about three inches deep. Compress the soil well around the cuttings and water. Keep well watered and fed throughout the growing season. Keep weeded during the first season; after that, it will pretty well take care of itself. You should be able to harvest your first horseradish roots in two to three years. Dig and cut the larger roots in the fall, leaving the smaller roots for regrowth of the plant. To use, peel and grate the roots. You can also dig roots to establish more plants if desired.

⊗ If you have the space you can grow your own horseradish. It does tend to spread so be sure to have a way to contain it if possible.

Ginger

One unusual perennial, although grown somewhat differently, is ginger. Ginger is a tropical plant that requires warm, moist growing conditions. You can, however, grow enough for flavoring indoors in pots. Purchase a ginger root at a grocery or Oriental food store, as the roots are not readily available from seed companies or garden centers. Plant the root in a six- to eight-inch container filled with a good potting soil.

Water well and place in a sunny south or west window. Keep well watered. If your house is dry, occasionally mist with a spray of water. When the root fills the pot, remove and cut off a two- to three-inch piece to restart. Keep the root in a dry place for use or slice and store in the freezer.

9

Herbs

You don't need to grow a huge garden to enjoy growing foods. Herbs are small-garden favorites. Some can even be grown in pots on your deck, patio, or window. Cooking with your own herbs adds personalized flavoring and spices to your dishes. Most herbs are fairly easy to grow, and many also add decor to your backyard or garden. Some herbs are grown as annuals, some as perennials. Annuals are available as seed, perennials as plants. Most herbs do best in full sun and in well-drained soil. Most seeds are planted one-fourth-inch deep, and seeds

⊗ Growing your own herbs, such as dill, is a fun and great way of adding excitement to your cooking.

⊗ Balm

and transplants should be keep well watered, at least one inch of water per week. Mulching can conserve moisture for garden-planted herbs. Make sure to keep the plants well weeded.

Mulch can also be a great help in weed control. If growing in a garden and if you're like me, you'll have trouble identifying the young seedlings. I prefer to start herb seeds indoors and then transplant, making it easier to identify the young plants. Perennials should be dug up and divided in the spring every three or four years. Cut away the outside clumps and replant; replant the main clump in the same area. The following are some favorite herbs and how to grow them:

Anise. Grow as an annual. Young leaves are used for garnishes, seeds for flavoring candy and cakes, as well

⊗ Borage

as ground for sachet powder. The distilled oil is used in perfumes.

Balm. Grow as a perennial. Leaves have a lemony fragrance and are sometimes used for flavoring stews and soups. Balm is also a honeybee attractant.

Basil. Grow as an annual. A wide range of different basils are available, each with a slightly different flavor. Sweet basil has a very aromatic, sweet, clovelike fragrance. Fresh basil leaves are used in stews, for flavoring salads, and in dressings. Dried leaves are used in sauces and in sausages.

Borage. Grow as an annual. Tender young leaves have a cucumber-like taste and are used in salads and to spice up lemonade. This is another plant honeybees love.

Catnip. Grow as an annual. This herb is most commonly made into a soothing tea. It's a member of the mint family and spreads rapidly. Cats and bees love it.

⌃ Caraway seeds

Caraway. Grow as an annual and as a biennial. Young leaves and shoots are used in salads. Seeds are the most important part of this herb. The distilled oil is used in flavoring cakes, candy, sauces, breads, and soups.

Chives. Grow as an annual or perennial. This herb belongs to the onion family but is less pungent.

⌄ Chives

⌄ Catnip

⊗ Many herbs, such as cilantro, are easily grown in pots or containers.

Chives are used to flavor soups, salads, and stir-fry. Some varieties also have a slight garlic flavor.

Cilantro. Grow as an annual. Also called Chinese or Mexican parsley, the leaves of cilantro are used as flavoring in popular ethnic dishes.

Coriander. Grow as an annual. Coriander is the dried seeds of the cilantro plant. They are used whole or ground in everything from meat dishes to desserts, soups and breads.

Dill. Grow as an annual. Seeds and stems are used in dill pickles, dill vinegar, and as a flavoring for stews, soups, and sauces.

Epazote. Grow as an annual. It is a spice used in Mexican bean dishes to prevent gas and indigestion.

Fennel. Grow as a perennial. The stem bases have an aniselike flavor. Leaves are used in fish and vegetable dishes. Seeds are used in soups, on baked goods, and in sausages.

Horehound. Grow as a perennial. It has an aromatic odor and pungent, bitter taste. It is often used as a tonic in cough syrups and, in large doses, is a laxative.

Lavender. Grow as a perennial or annual. The dried leaves and flowers are used in potpourri and sachets.

⊗ Coriander

⊗ Fennel

❤ Lavender

❤ Marjoram

Marjoram, sweet. Grow as a perennial. Young leaves and stems are used fresh or dried in fish and meat sauces, dressings and stews.

Oregano. Grow as an annual. Strongly aromatic leaves are used dried or fresh in tomato-based sauces,

❤ Oregano

❤ Rosemary

salads, meat and fish dishes, and in Italian dishes.

Rosemary. Grow as a perennial. Young leaves and stems are used fresh or dried to flavor fish and meat dishes.

Sage. Grow as an annual or perennial. The extremely aromatic leaves

❤ Sage

❄ Mint

are used both fresh and dried for sea-
soning meats, especially pork sausage.
Also used as a spice in turkey stuffing.

❄ Basil

❄ Thyme

❄ Summer savory

⊗ Some herbs are annuals, some perennials. It's important to know how to start and grow each.

Spearmint. Grow as an annual or perennial. Has a fresh aroma popular for use in candies, jellies, and drinks.

Summer savory. Grow as an annual. The leaves and stems are used both fresh and dried in meat sauces and stews. Summer savory is also called the bean herb because it's often used as a flavoring in lentil bean dishes.

Thyme. Grow as an annual or perennial. The leaves and stems are used fresh and dried in meat sauces, poultry dishes, and in sausages.

The leaves and stems of many herbs are simply snipped off as needed to flavor dishes. You can keep many herbs growing all winter in pots indoors or a greenhouse for a continuous supply of flavorings. Most herbs should be harvested just before the flowers open, including marjoram, summer savory, basil, sage, oregano, mint, and fennel. Thyme and rosemary can be harvested when plants are in full bloom.

Herbs can also be dried for future use. To dry, loosely tie the herb stems in bundles and hang in a cool, dark room with plenty of ventilation. Or you can spread the herbs out on cheesecloth to dry. In this case, check regularly and stir frequently to make sure mold doesn't form. You can also use a food dehydrator to speed up the process. Store dried herbs in airtight containers in a cool, dark area.

10

Small Fruits

Small fruits, including raspberries, blackberries, blueberries, strawberries, and grapes, are some of the most satisfying and rewarding foods to grow. Growing the volume of small fruits for a family to eat fresh and preserved, however, requires a fairly large area. The mouthwatering flavor of homegrown berries and the savings from growing your own are reasons enough to grow as much as space allows. All the small fruits are extremely good for you and low in calories.

The following are the most common small fruits and how to grow them:

❁ Growing your own small fruits, such as strawberries, is very satisfying, a great budget extender, and a way of providing your family with lots of healthy foods.

Strawberries

Strawberries are the most popular small fruit. Some growing methods are primarily for commercial productions and can be labor intensive and discouraging to the first-timer or home food grower. Newer growing methods make growing strawberries easier and more productive.

Strawberries are basically short-lived perennials. Some traditional strawberry varieties take a year for the plants to reach bearing size, and then they will produce for a couple of seasons. As they grow, the plants send out runners to create new or "daughter" plants. A traditional established bed consists of three different types of plants—plants not yet bearing but still growing, plants in full production, and plants that have stopped bearing. This makes growing strawberries a bit complicated for the first-timer. Strawberries also require patience when grown traditionally, as it takes at least two years to get a productive crop.

A wide range of strawberry varieties are available with differing qualities. The berries of some varieties have the firmness needed for shipping and the large size needed by commercial growers. Other qualities include berries best for freezing, berries for preserves and jam, berries that do best in poor or dry soils, as well as berries for very cold climates. There are also early midseason and late-bearing varieties. If all that isn't confusing enough, strawberries are also available as June bearers, ever bearing, and the newer day neutral.

June-bearing strawberries ripen in late May and June and produce a good main crop for processing. These berries are managed to produce a crop the following or second season after planting. All blossoms are removed the first year. Runners creating daughter plants fill in the matted row.

Ever-bearing plants can often be productive in the fall following a

⊗ Strawberries are a very popular small fruit to grow in a home garden.

spring planting. In the second season, ever-bearing strawberries are productive in both spring and fall. Ever bearers, however, are not as productive as June bearers, but produce some berries throughout the season. Ever bearers are easier to grow and are often used in deck planters, strawberry barrels, and pyramid plantings. The berries are usually smaller than the June bearers.

Day-neutral strawberries are grown much different than both the June bearers and the older, more traditional ever-bearing varieties. Day-neutral berries produce fruit throughout the season, producing flower buds continuously as long as the temperature is not too high (above 85°F). Day-neutral berries are normally productive during the year of planting. They also produce the second year and then are replanted. It's important to pinch off all runners as they form. When all the runners are pinched off, new plants must be purchased to replenish the bed. For bigger berries, pinch off the first blossoms for a week or so and then let the berries form. These berries typically make their best production the fall following the initial planting.

It's important to match the berries to your locale. Check with your local cooperative extension office as to the best varieties for your area. Always purchase disease-free, certified virus-free plants. You'll need about twenty-five plants to start a strawberry bed for a family of four.

Strawberries have traditionally been planted in three systems: the hill system, matted rows, and spaced rows.

Spaced row strawberries

pinch all but two runners

◉ Strawberries are planted in one of three systems. This is a spaced row.

Strawberry hill system

keep plants pinched back to single plants

◉ Above is a hill system.

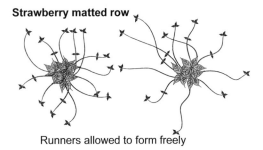

Strawberry matted row

Runners allowed to form freely

❷ Above is a matted row system.

The hill system is best for those with limited space but is not as productive over time. Set the plants twelve to eighteen inches apart in all directions. Remove all runners as they form. This is a good system for small beds, producing a few choice berries for fresh eating. In cool climate areas, the hill system is often used in conjunction with black plastic mulch to warm the ground and extend the growing.

The most common planting system for more production is the old-time matted row. The plants are set twelve to twenty-four inches apart in rows four feet apart. All the runners are allowed to grow and are spaced outward to create a wide matted row. This is an easy method, and also less time-consuming because weeding is cut down by the strawberry foliage.

The spaced-row system is a good choice for home gardeners. They are planted in the same manner as for a matted row, except the runners are thinned as soon as they form until about mid-June, creating plants spaced six to seven inches apart. This produces the best, high-quality biggest fruit.

Strawberries have specific requirements to be productive. They need a sunny area with a rich, well-drained soil. Although the plants are extremely hardy, the blossoms are very easily damaged by spring frosts. The upper side of a slight slope is a good choice. Growing strawberries in raised beds is an excellent idea for the home food grower. The raised beds are easier to work and maintain; it's easier to create the deep, rich soil; and more importantly, it's easier to battle the weeds. Weeds are the bane of the strawberry grower. Don't simply dig up turf and start a strawberry patch. You'll be fighting weeds forever. If you've ever tried to keep quack grass or crabgrass out of a strawberry bed, you'll know utter frustration.

Prepare the bed in late summer or early fall for a spring planting if possible, although the bed can be prepared in early spring in some areas. Till, dig, spade, whatever is needed to deeply

⊗ Strawberries require a sunny spot with well-drained soil. A raised bed can be extremely productive.

⊗ Strawberry plants come as transplants that must be set out.

break up the soil. Although strawberries like well-drained soil, it must also hold some moisture. Add plenty of organic matter. Layer rotted manure, compost, peat moss, and other materials over the bed. About two bushels of manure per one hundred square feet of bed are needed. Till and mix to a depth of six to eight inches. If preparing the bed in fall, spread light straw mulch over the bed for the winter. This will keep the soil loose and friable, ready for easy planting in the spring.

A rich, deep bed probably won't need much fertilizer at planting time, but strawberries need nutrients. A general-purpose fertilizer, such as 12-12-12, or cottonseed meal, fish meal, and a little wood ash should be applied about two weeks after planting. Apply one-half cup of 12-12-12 per twenty-five feet of row. Side-dress with the same amount twice more during the year. I usually apply a water-soluble fertilizer with a soaker hose.

In most parts of the country, strawberries are set out in early spring, about the same time as cabbage transplants, or a few weeks before the last frost. Strawberry plants are sold in bunches from mail-order nurseries and garden centers. Set out the plants as soon as you receive or purchase them. If you can't plant them immediately, place them in the crisper drawer of your refrigerator. Wrap the roots with damp paper towels. You can also keep the plants in a shallow trench in a shady spot in your garden. Cover the roots with soil.

The best time to set out plants is a quiet, overcast day. If it's hot, wait until late afternoon. Examine the plants and discard any that are moldy or dark. Place the roots in a container of water while you work. Strawberries must be planted at the right depth.

The plant consists of roots, a crown or the center bulging portion of the plant, and the leaves. The plants must be set with the roots well covered, but the crown at ground level.

The traditional method of planting is to dig a hole big enough to spread out the roots, water, and set the plant at the correct depth with the roots fanned out. Compress the soil down and around the roots and up to the crown level and then water again. Adding a teaspoon of water-soluble fertilizer to a gallon of water and using for the last step will help get the plants off to a good start.

If using the hill system, mulch around the plants. If using the matted or spaced row, don't mulch. Instead, till or hoe shallowly around the plants. This keeps the weeds out and the soil loose and friable for easier rooting of daughter plants. Train the runners to fill in where you want them by positioning them and then placing small stones or clods of dirt on the stems. Now comes the hard part with traditional matted or spaced-row June-bearer plants—pick off all the blossoms on the first season. Nope, no strawberries the first year. This allows the plants to put all

❷ The plants must be set at the proper depth

Crown

Correct

Too high

Too low

⊗ Dig a small hole, make a slight raised cone in the center, spread the roots out over the cone, and fill in around the roots with soil.

their energy into growing a full bed. Ever bearers only need to be pruned of blossoms until midsummer and then berries can be picked that fall.

In late August or early September, side-dress with a general-purpose

⊗ Water well.

fertilizer. This puts nutrients into producing next year's berries. Side-dressing early in the spring tends to put the energy into producing more foliage.

After a few frosts in late fall but before the temperature drops below 20°F, cover the plants with four to five inches of good mulch. Make sure the mulch is weed-seed free. Straw is usually the best choice or wood chips or sawdust. Early the next spring, rake off about half the mulch, leaving some around the plants, and spread between the rows. Leave about a two-inch layer of mulch for the rest of the season. The plants will grow through the mulch, yet it will help keep the weeds down. That's the biggest problem with these methods—you will still have weeds. Some growers utilize herbicides, but I prefer to weed by hand, although it can be work.

⊗ In late fall cover the plants with mulch.

⊗ Rake back the mulch in the early spring.

Strawberries are luscious and juicy, and for that reason, they need lots of water, at least one inch per week. If you don't get that through rain, you'll have to irrigate. Set an empty can in the bed to indicate how much rain you're getting or how much from irrigation. During the growing season, I like to apply a water-soluble fertilizer as I water once a week. During hot weather, I may irrigate more often.

After the second growing season, many growers simply till in the plants and start again. For this reason, you may prefer to have two beds, rotating the beds to keep a regular supply of berries. The traditional matted-row method of renovation is used commercially and on larger beds. Immediately after harvest, narrow the row to six to twelve inches in width. Rake out any dead leaves and pull all weeds. Thin the plants in the row to six to nine inches apart. Mow over the bed with the mower set one to three inches above the tops of the crowns. On raised beds, carefully use a string trimmer. Apply a light covering of compost or well-rotted manure. Side-dress with fertilizer and water the plants. Keep the bed weeded or apply a pre-emergent herbicide. Cover with mulch in the fall. Daughter plants can be dug up and planted in another bed for a continuous supply of plants. I also dig some of the daughter plants in the fall and heel them over in trenches in the garden for a new bed the following spring.

⊗ Monte's easy-does-it strawberry method uses black plastic around the plants, with wood-chip mulch over the plastic.

Monte's easy-does-it strawberry method comes from several years of strawberry hassle. Two beds holding twenty-five plants each will produce an abundance of fresh berries, frozen berries, and preserves. The beds are raised beds, and the soil is well prepared and fertilized. A soaker hose is laid down the center of each bed and a layer of weed-barrier fabric stapled to the top of the wooden edges of the raised beds. The plants are planted in slits in the fabric. Once the plants are established, sawdust mulch is applied over the fabric. There are no weeds, the beds stay moist but not soaking, and strawberries are available from fall to the second year with ever bearers and throughout the first year with day-neutral berries. After two years, the beds are started over. Make sure you keep strawberries well picked to keep a continuous crop growing.

Blueberries

Another small-fruit favorite is blueberries. These delicious and, in the supermarket, extremely expensive small fruits are not only a tasty treat but are also very good for you. Although blueberries have some fairly

⊗ Blueberries are another small fruit favorite that are really good for you.

stringent requirements, with a little effort some varieties can be grown almost anywhere. Blueberries not only provide food but also a great backyard ornamental plant as well, adding color all season long. Blueberries require an acidic soil, at least a 160-day growing season, and winters no colder than $-20°$ to $-25°F$. A number of varieties are available with some bred for northern and some for southern gardens. Blueberries are relatively easy to grow once established and are very easy to pick and preserve. Blueberries are available as early-, midseason, and late-season varieties. A couple of plants of each will provide plenty of delicious berries both fresh and frozen. You will need at least two varieties for pollination.

Blueberry plants may be set out in late fall or early spring. Make sure you purchase disease-free plants. Blueberry plants may be purchased as rooted cuttings, bare-rooted plants, and potted plants. The best choices for most purposes are the two- to three-year-old plants normally sold as bare rooted by mail order or potted in nurseries. Although a bit more costly, they usually have better plant survival and get off to an earlier start.

The ideal blueberry-growing soil has a continuous water supply because of the shallow roots yet is well drained,

⊗ Blueberry plants are available bare root or potted. The first step is to dig a hole large enough to accommodate the roots and also to incorporate the addition of peat moss and some compost.

has lots of organic matter, and is acidic. Space plants four feet apart in rows eight to ten feet apart. To prepare for blueberry plants, dig a hole twelve to fifteen inches deep and large

⊗ Blueberries require an acidic soil. Add sphagnum peat moss to the planting hole.

⊗ Set the plant in place and compress the soil around the plant.

⊗ Water well, then mulch around the plant with wood chips.

enough to hold the spread-out roots. Mix a half bushel of wet sphagnum peat moss with coarse sand and mix that in with some compost or good garden soil. Spread a layer of the mix in the bottom of the hole, spread out the blueberry roots laterally, add more of the soil mix, and compress the soil down around the roots.

If setting out potted plants, make shallow vertical cuts in the ball of roots to allow the roots to spread into the surrounding soil.

Good permanent mulch at least four to six inches deep around and between the plants is extremely important for blueberries. Hay, straw, pine needles, or the best wood chips or sawdust, which doesn't break down quite as rapidly, are all good. One method of keeping a continuous water supply during dry weather is to run a soaker hose alongside the plants and cover the hose with mulch. It takes a lot of mulch to maintain blueberries, and you will need to add more each year.

Blueberries are fairly heavy feeders and require annual applications of either organic or synthetic fertilizer. An application of a general-purpose fertilizer (12-12-12) should be applied four to six weeks after spring-planted

⊗ Blueberries are fairly heavy feeders. Apply fertilizer on established plants before the blossoms open each spring.

blueberries. Use two tablespoons spread evenly around each plant. About six weeks later, fertilize using one tablespoon of ammonium sulfate per plant to help keep the pH level down.

Water-soluble fertilizers for acid-loving plants can also be used. During the second growing season, when the buds begin to break in the spring, fertilize with four tablespoons of general-purpose fertilizer per plant, followed six weeks later by two table-spoons ammonium sulfate per plant. Continue the ammonium sulfate applications at six-week intervals. For established plants, three years or older, apply one-half cup 13-13-13 at bud break in the spring, followed by

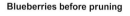

⊗ Blueberries must be pruned properly to continue production. Before.

Blueberries before pruning

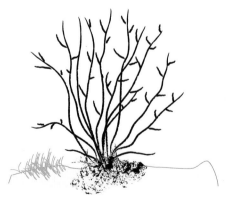

Blueberries after pruning

⊗ After.

one-fourth cup ammonium sulfate six weeks later. Continue the ammonium sulfate at six week intervals two more times during the season.

High bush blueberries are highly prolific and require pruning. Blueberries produce fruit on the previous year's wood. Prune in early spring, usually February or March before the buds break. Prune very lightly during the first and second seasons, removing only dead or broken branches. Prune lightly during the third and fourth seasons as well, cutting out dead and broken branches and stems and removing a few of the thin, spindly growth from the previous season. By the fifth season, more serious pruning is required. In addition to cutting away dead and damaged growth, cut out the weakest youngest stems from the previous season and remove about one-fifth of the oldest-producing canes from the base.

Brambles

Other favored small fruits are blackberries and raspberries. They can also be grown at home for delicious pies, jams, jellies, and to be simply eaten fresh. Brambles are very easy to grow and, in fact, will often spread and take over an area.

⊗ Brambles, such as blackberries and raspberries, are easy to grow but do take up space.

⊗ It's important to plant brambles at the proper depth.

Brambles

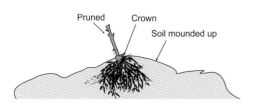

Brambles are available in a number of varieties both as trailing and upright berries. Their requirements are similar. All require a deep loamy soil with lots of organic material. Brambles won't tolerate heavy or poorly draining soil. Both blackberries and raspberries like lots of sun, although raspberries can be grown in sun to partial shade. It's important to properly prepare the planting site. Dig a hole that will accommodate the roots and is twice as deep as needed. Add a layer of compost or good garden soil to the hole. Water and set the plants in place. Do not plant too deep; the crown of the plant should be at soil level.

The roots should be just under the surface. If setting out potted plants, plant at the same depth they were in the pot. Water and make sure the soil is firmed around the roots. For bare-root plants, prune the canes back to about two inches. You won't need to prune potted plants. Fertilizer isn't required the first year, but mulch the plants heavily and keep them well watered and weeded. An application of 10-10-10 or other general-purpose plant fertilizer can be applied the next spring and each spring thereafter.

Before pruning

after pruning

⊗ After.

⊗ Proper pruning is also needed for blackberries. Before.

Blackberries are available in the traditional thorny and thornless varieties. New varieties such as Prime-Jan and Prime-Jim are totally different from traditional varieties. Most berries produce on last year's canes. The new varieties bear on both last year's canes as well as the new canes. This not only prevents frost from getting the berries in northern parts of the country but also spreads the harvest throughout the season. Blackberries and boysenberries should be spaced five feet apart for upright varieties and eight feet apart for trailing varieties. Rows should be eight feet apart. Cut off or pinch off buds the first year so fruits won't set. Blackberries must be pruned annually and properly to be productive. After the plants are established, prune in the spring. Prune away old, weak, and dead wood. Cut all but the heaviest canes to the ground. Leave the heavy canes spaced about six to eight inches apart. Prune back the tips, leaving about ten to twelve buds per cane. Tie canes to wires or other supports if desired.

Raspberries are available in a number of varieties, producing some of the tastiest homegrown fruits. Raspberries are available in black, purple, red, and gold; and in summer- bearing- and fall- or ever-bearing varieties. Plant raspberries in rows with plants spaced two feet apart for purple and red summer-bearing berries and one foot apart for fall- or ever-bearing berries. Leave at least eight feet between rows. Set out raspberries as soon as the ground can be worked on. Water and make sure soil is firmed around the plants. Once the plants are set, cut the canes down to ground level and apply mulch. Remove all cut

❷ Raspberries are available in a number of varieties, including black, red, and gold.

canes from the area. Raspberry diseases spread rapidly. One month after planting apply one cup of a general-purpose fertilizer per ten feet of row or about five plants. The first year after planting, apply one cup of fertilizer per ten-foot row in March. In succeeding years, apply two cups of general-purpose fertilizer per ten feet of row in March.

Prune summer-bearing raspberries in January or February, removing any damaged or spindly canes. Thin to three or four canes per foot. Trim the tops of the canes to about five feet high but do not remove more than one-fourth of each cane. Immediately following harvest remove the canes that bore fruit. Again, cut out all damaged or spindly canes. Remove all trimmings and cuttings from pruning and burn.

Prune fall- and ever-bearing raspberries to produce a fall crop by cutting all canes down close to the ground in January or February. Do not damage the crowns. Make sure to remove all trimmings and burn.

Black and purple raspberries produce fruit on side branches or laterals. To induce more fruiting, cut the tips off the primocanes throughout

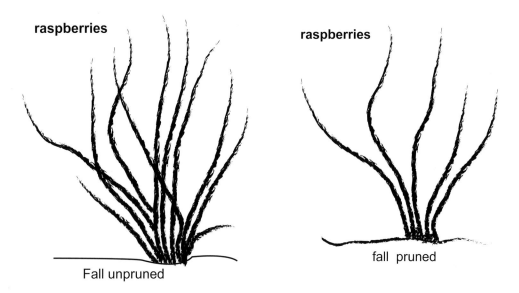

raspberries

Fall unpruned

raspberries

fall pruned

❂ Raspberries also need proper pruning, the appropriate method depending on whether the berries are summer or fall bearing. The above drawings show fall bearing pruned (before and after).

the summer of the first year, reducing black raspberry canes to twenty-four inches and purple to thirty inches. This promotes the development of the side branches that will bear fruit the following year. After the harvest in subsequent years, continue to summer-trim the primocanes. Cut the

❂ The below drawings show summer bearing pruned (before and after).

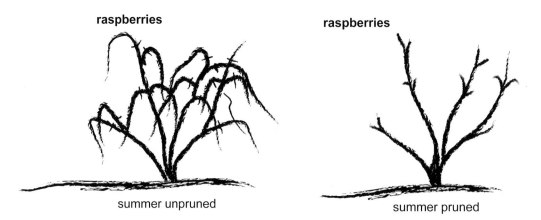

raspberries

summer unpruned

raspberries

summer pruned

fruit-producing canes to ground level. In February, cut back the laterals to eight to twelve inches. Thin the canes to four to six per plant.

Grapes

Grapes take more time and effort to get started and also more effort in management. Grapes must be trained on trellises to keep the fruit off the ground and provide air circulation. They must be pruned properly in order to produce. Birds may be a problem, requiring netting to protect the fruit. Grapes, however, have been a tradition in many a backyard. The popular Concord grapes are relatively easy to grow and produce the old-time standard eating grape, juice, and jellies. Most grape varieties bear fruit within two years, with each plant producing about fifteen pounds of fruit per year. You will need about eight feet of trellis for each plant.

Grapes are available in a wide range of varieties and in red, white, and blue types. All varieties of grapes can't be grown successfully in all parts of the country. It's important to grow

A grape arbor was a tradition on many homesteads and in many backyards. You can grow your own grapes for juice, jelly, or wine.

the varieties that adapt to your geographic region and climate. Growers in the northeast and upper Midwest must choose varieties hardy enough to withstand extreme cold winters or hardy to −30° or −40°F. For the most part, American cultivars are hardier than the French-American varieties. Ripening times also vary, from midsummer through fall. Check with your local cooperative extension office as to varieties that do best in your area.

As with most plants, grapes have specific requirements, with the planting site the most important. Grapes need full sun, good air circulation, a well-drained area, and one without late-spring frosts. Most people don't think of Missouri as a grape-growing state, but it has lots of wineries and grape growers. Much of the state is hilly, especially the southern area or Ozarks where we live, and the hillsides are ideal for grape production. An ideal site is the top or upper slope facing south or east. North- and west-facing slopes don't receive full sun until later in the day, which allows dew to stay on the plants longer. Good air circulation is extremely important to help prevent fungus growth, a grape

bane. If possible, run the grape rows parallel to the prevailing winds to allow the wind to help dry the grape foliage after rains and dew.

Space the grapes according to the type. Most grapes should be planted eight feet apart with ten feet between rows. Muscatine grapevines should be spaced twelve to fifteen feet apart. Most grapevines are purchased as bare-root cuttings. Inspect the cuttings. Roots that are dark brownish, soft, and spongy may have been frozen and may rot. Cut off dead or broken shoots. Soak the roots in water for a few hours and plant as soon as possible. Keep the plants moist while setting them out. Dig the planting hole large enough to accommodate all the roots without crowding or bending them. Work plenty of organic matter in with the soil from the hole. Mix a bit of compost or well-rotted manure

☯ **It's important to set out grape plants properly.**

Planting grapes

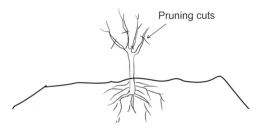

Pruning cuts

in with the garden soil. In the bottom of the hole, create a small mound of the loosened soil and compost and set the roots on the mound. You'll notice a dark area or nursery soil line on the trunk of the vine. Set the plant slightly deeper than this soil line. Make sure all roots are well spread out and then fill in over the roots. Add a bit of the soil/compost mix and water well. Add the remainder of the soil/compost mix, compress the soil, and water again. Prune the top of the vine to one stem containing three to four buds. Buds are the enlarged areas along the vine. Shallow cultivation during the first part of the growing season and mulch during the summer months will get your plants off to a great start. Do not fertilize new plantings until growth has begun and then use three

tablespoons of a general-purpose fertilizer such as 12-12-12. Scatter this in a two-foot-diameter circle around each plant but maintain a six-inch space around the trunk. Repeat a couple of times the first two months, spreading the fertilizer in wider circles, thirty-six and forty-eight inches around the vines. After the third year, apply the same type of fertilizer in March or early April at the rate of one and a half cups per vine.

Grapes need a trellis, arbor, or other support with a two-wire trellis the most common support. Grapes must also be trained onto the trellis. The traditional four-cane Kniffen method is the most common and best for home growers. It takes three years to train the plants onto the trellis. During the first year, the plants probably won't grow enough to begin training. At the start of the second year, begin training the vine onto the support. Keep the main trunk pruned to about four and a half feet high. Two shoots are trained to each of the wires in a T-fashion. Tie the shoots in place with something soft enough not to damage the vines. Beginning in the third year, shoots will be going in every direction. In late winter or early spring, prune heavily. Pick the four best

⊗ Grape plants must be trained to a trellis, and pruned properly and annually.

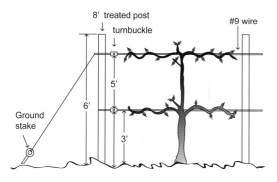

pencil-sized stems as the fruiting canes. Prune each back to eight or ten buds and tie to the wires. Next to the base of these stems, leave two short stems with at least two buds each. These will form the fruiting canes for the following year. Trim away all other stems. It sounds drastic, but you must do this each year in order for your vines to produce properly.

11

The Home Orchard

Growing fruits in your backyard is not only possible but also a great way of providing your family with wholesome foods. Nothing tastes better than a fresh peach picked from your own tree or a fresh steaming hot apple pie from your orchard. If you envision an orchard as acres of trees in rows, think again. Very productive orchards can be grown in very small spaces. With miniature and Colonnade trees from Stark Bro's, full-sized fruits can be grown on a balcony, patio, or sliver of ground. The backyard, however, is the place most of us grow fruit trees,

» You can grow fruits in your own home orchard, eating fresh and canning or preserving the excess, such as this peach jam.

and these days, even that doesn't have to be large to produce an abundance of delicious fruits.

Planning

As with a food garden, the home orchard shouldn't be so big it can't be taken care of properly. On the other hand, the orchard should be large enough to produce fruit for your family, both fresh and processed. An orchard requires space and, as with growing any foods, work. Any size of orchard requires yearly work. A poorly maintained orchard is not only unproductive, but it can also become an eyesore. Fruit trees must be spaced properly to produce, so the orchard size will need to match your space. Fruit trees are available in several sizes: standard, semidwarf, dwarf, and even miniature. Each matures to a different size.

The crowns or tops of standard trees mature to around twenty feet in diameter. Semidwarfs grow to around fifteen feet, dwarfs to ten feet, and miniatures to six feet in diameter. Standard trees can grow well over twenty-five feet tall. Semidwarfs typically grow fifteen to seventeen feet, and dwarfs seven to ten feet tall. Spacing between the trees is needed to assure good sunlight and air circulation. Just because the trees are smaller doesn't mean they aren't productive. Semidwarf

❂ A home orchard takes work but it not only adds to your stock of homegrown food but the beauty of your backyard as well.

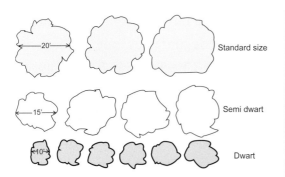

⊗ A home-orchard should be carefully planned and spaced for productivity and to increase the value of your property.

⊗ Some fruits are easier to grow than others in certain locales. For instance apricots are hard to grow in certain areas.

and dwarf trees can produce plenty of fruits for the home orchard. They also produce quicker than standard-size trees, although they don't live as long. Keep in mind that many trees require a second variety planted close at hand as a pollinator. Nut trees typically are only standard size. They take up a lot of space, and it takes a good number of years for them to produce. You might consider carefully before using limited orchard space for nut trees. The chart shows the time, estimated yield of the different trees, as well as time from planting to harvest.

Species, time from planting to harvest, life in years, and estimated annual yield are listed below:

Apple

Standard: 4 to 6 years, 35 to 45, 10 to 15 bu. per tree

⊗ A wide range of fruits can be homegrown including apples.

Semidwarf: 3 to 5, 20 to 30, 6 to 10 bu. per tree

Dwarf: 2 to 4, 15 to 20, 3 to 6 bu. per tree

Pear

Standard: 5 to 8 years, 35 to 40, 10 to 15 bu. per tree

Semidwarf: 3 to 5, 20 to 30, 5 to 10 bu. per tree

Peach

Standard: 2 to 4 years, 15 to 20, 3 to 8 bu. per tree

Semidwarf: 1 to 2, 10 to 15, 1 to 3 bu. per tree

Plum 4 to 6 years 15 to 20 3.5 bu. per tree

Pie cherry 3 to 5 years, 15 to 20, 2 to 3 bu. per tree

A wide range of fruit varieties are available both by mail order and from local nurseries. It's important to pick varieties that will do well in your area.

Some fruit trees are quite specific in their needs and may not produce in your area. Check nursery catalogs for zone and climate requirements. It's also a good idea to check with your local cooperative extension office as to the best varieties for your area.

⊗ Pears

⊗ Plums

⊗ Peaches

Location

Picking the correct location for your orchard or individual fruit trees is extremely important. An orchard should have plenty of sun and a well-drained, fertile soil. You'll need at least six to eight hours of sunlight. Higher elevations are also better than lower, as lower elevations tend to have later spring frosts, which can destroy blossoms. An east or south-facing, gently sloping hillside is the best choice. Soils can be amended somewhat and fertilizer applied to grow your trees, but soils with very poor drainage or of heavy clay should be avoided.

Careful planning is extremely important. Once planted, fruit trees are a permanent fixture, as I learned the hard way several years ago after planting a fruit tree where we later needed to place a driveway. In addition to producing fruit, the tree can also be a landscaping feature or nightmare. Determine the location of your tree or trees and try to imagine it as a full-grown tree. Look at the surroundings. Are there sidewalks nearby, overhead lines, possibly buried cables, sewer lines, or water pipes? Will it obstruct your vision of areas you want to see? Plant at least ten to twelve feet away from patios and sewer and waterlines. The roots tend to grow to water and can cause serious problems. Also check for shade trees, buildings, or other objects that might shade your new trees. In many instances, once you discover the pleasure and advantages of a home orchard, you may wish to expand, so plan for future trees as well. Make up an orchard plan on grid paper. Measure the area and mark the location of important features, buildings, patios, utilities, and so forth. Then draw circles of the correct size of mature trees in possible locations. With the plan in hand, use stakes to mark out locations of the trees. To make sure you plant the trees in the exact locations of the stakes, use a planting board. Position the board with its notch in the tree location stake. Then drive stakes at the notches in either end. The outside

stakes mark the outside edges of the planting hole.

Planting

Fruit trees can be planted either spring or fall. Both times have advantages. Fall trees don't have to fight the weeds, insects, and possible summer drought, but they typically don't really make any growth until the following spring. Spring is the usual planting time. Regardless, if possible, plant your new trees as soon as you purchase or receive them. This will help the roots get off to a healthy start. I like to have my planting holes dug, everything on hand, and be ready for my new trees. If you can't plant immediately, the trees can be stored for a short period. Open the package and wrap the tree roots in damp newspaper and then rewrap the roots and newspaper covering back in the packing plastic. Store the dampened roots in a cool place such as a basement. Dampen the roots again every couple of days. If you must keep the trees longer, they can be "heeled in" in a shallow trench in your garden. Again, keep the roots watered.

Soak the roots for twelve to twenty-four hours before planting. Keep the roots wet with damp newspapers while planting to protect from sun and wind. The most important factor in planting, however, is the hole. The hole must be large enough so the roots are not crowded and deep enough to be able to set the plant one-inch deeper than the nursery soil line. In many instances, you may need to amend the soil, adding compost or, in the case of heavy clay soil, about a third peat. Mix well with the planting soil. In heavy clay soil, dig the hole about double the recommended size. Use the planting board and stakes to determine the size of the hole. Fill the hole about one-third with well-pulverized or amended soil. Set the tree in place, making sure the nursery-soil line is at the right height. Spread out the roots.

❷ Fruit trees must be planted properly.

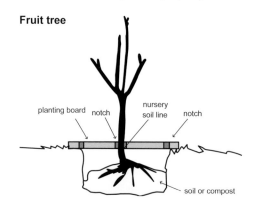

Fruit tree

planting board   notch   nursery soil line   notch

soil or compost

Use the notched board across the hole to determine the correct height. Note that grafted trees require a somewhat different method, leaving the bud union aboveground. Follow planting instructions that came with your tree. Add soil to fill the hole to about three-fourths full and tamp the soil firmly around the roots. Pour in a bucket of water and allow it to soak in. Some nurseries sell special time-release tree fertilizer to be applied at this time. No other fertilizers, however, should be applied. After the water has soaked in, fill the hole with the remainder of the soil, leaving a slight depression around the tree trunk. This allows water to stand and soak in around the tree and down to the roots. In the fall, fill in this indentation to prevent water from collecting and freezing around the trunk and roots. Spread mulch around the tree to help conserve moisture and keep down weeds.

In some cases, nursery stock, such as fruit trees, are prepruned for planting. In other instances, pruning may be needed at planting time. Follow the instructions with your tree for specific pruning details at planting time. Make sure to soak the soil frequently and thoroughly throughout the first growing season. Note that some dormant or bare-root stock may take quite a bit of time to get started. Be patient. If you're in doubt, scratch a tiny area of bark with your fingernail. If the tree is green underneath, it's alive.

Staking can help young trees get off to a good start and prevent wind damage. In our part of the country, deer and rabbits are a serious problem. Deer eat the young leaves, and bucks rub off the bark. Rabbits nibble the bark off the trunk. Wrapping the trunk with heavy paper is one method of preventing the trunk problems. Special tree-trunk guards are also available. My tactic is to stake the tree, add mulch, and use a cage, much like a tomato cage around the tree. The cage is also staked in place to prevent being blown or pushed over. You may wish to paint the lower trunk and crotch with a good-quality water-soluble white paint. This reduces the problems of winter injury from the heat of the sun, creating bark splitting and other damage. The paint can be indoor or outdoor and should be thinned half with water. Do not use oil-based paints, as they can kill the tree.

Maintenance

Fruit trees require quite a bit of maintenance in order to be productive. This includes regular watering, some fertilizing, and most importantly, proper pruning. You will need at least an inch of water every ten days to two weeks. In times of drought, make sure to keep your tree well watered. One method is to use a garden hose set to lightly trickle. If you have several trees, a soaker hose is a good idea. I've reworked sections of soaker and solid garden hose from old hoses to create hose spacing for my trees and easy watering, a must in our hot, dry Ozark summers. Don't overwater. Frequently drowning the roots is a definite no-no. Keep the area around the trees well mulched to protect the roots, control weeds, and keep moisture in place. Use leaves, straw, or wood chips. Before winter, rake the mulch back away from the trunk so mice won't nest near the trunk.

Fruit trees require fertilization but, in most instances, in specific and differing amounts. You can use general-purpose fertilizers or special orchard fertilizers. Again, follow instructions for your particular variety of tree as

⊗ To be productive, the home orchard requires yearly maintenance including regular feeding and watering.

⊗ As you can imagine, fruit trees are susceptible to lots of pest, including bugs and critters.

to types of fertilizer, amount, and timing.

Pests

As you can imagine, just about everything that walks, flies, or crawls loves fruit trees and the fruits. There are numerous ways to handle the problems, including mechanical, with organic, or chemical means. We use as much mechanical means as possible. Squirrels are a major problem with apricots. They don't eat the fruits, but chew through the fruits to get the seeds, which taste like almonds. We tried any number of means of fighting these pests and finally solved the problem with aluminum tree guards placed around the trunk of the trees. The same method kept the raccoons out of the pear trees, after years of

⊗ Keep your orchard clean. Pick off all mummified fruits and destroy them immediately.

fighting that problem as well. Birds can really be a problem, especially with cherries and apricots, but garden nets stretched over the trees can solve that problem.

A clean orchard is the first step in fighting disease and insects. Make sure to keep the trees pruned properly, cutting away dead, diseased, and

⊗ The most important pruning steps involve cutting away dead and diseased branches, as well as keeping the center of the tree open.

⊗ For the most part it's important to use some sort of protection from pests and diseases on your orchard trees.

damaged limbs. Burn the discards to prevent spreading diseases. Remove and burn any "mummified" fruits on the trees or any that may have dropped on the ground. Mow and rake the ground around the trees to remove any debris.

Most orchards, especially commercial orchards, rely heavily on pesticide sprays, and if you want perfect and bountiful fruit, it's required. We tend to use a variety of pest-control methods. Our apple orchard consists of about twenty trees, and the only chemical used on it is a dormant-oil spray in late spring/early summer.

No, the apples are not perfect; they have splotches, black spots, and some insect damage. But the orchard produces a bounty of delicious apples, and we don't mind the "ugly" apples. We also don't spray our pears. On the other hand, we use some sprays on our peaches, although organic methods are available.

Spraying pesticides should not be taken lightly. You can cause serious damage to yourself, even be killed if you don't follow all safety precautions. As a farmer, I've had to be certified to use certain chemicals, although I rarely and prefer not to use them.

The class is a day-long affair and serious business and is required before purchasing some chemicals.

Safety Rules

Read the label before opening the container. Note all warnings, precautions, and antidotes. If the label suggests a respirator, goggles, rubber gloves, and clothing, you're better off leaving it alone. Most orchard sprays, however, are not that toxic but must still be carefully used.

☻ **Make sure to follow all safety rules when spraying chemicals.**

Measure accurately. Mix all ingredients on a solid level surface to prevent spilling. If you get concentrate on your hands or body, wash immediately with soap and water. If you spill it on your clothing, change clothes and immediately launder the clothing.

Do not smoke or eat while mixing or spraying, or if your hands are contaminated. Wash hands immediately after using chemicals.

Cover bird baths, dog dishes, and fish pools. Don't leave pools of chemicals dogs or cats may be attracted to.

Don't spray when temperatures or winds are high. Spray in the early morning and late afternoon. Avoid drift and by all means do not let spray drift onto you.

Don't store leftover diluted spray. Spray left in the sprayer should be poured into a pit and covered over. Properly discard empty pesticide containers according to the instructions on the label.

Store pesticides in their original containers only. They should be kept in a locked cabinet away from children and pets.

Use the proper spraying equipment and make sure it is working correctly.

For correct spraying, a fruit-tree schedule should be followed. There are four basic stages of fruit-tree spray: dormant, prebloom, bloom, and petal fall. The timing of applications depends on the tree variety and the chemical used. And this is fairly detailed. Charts detailing the type of spray and timing for each type of fruit are available at your local cooperative extension office, from chemical companies, or online.

⊘ **Proper pruning is also important for continued productivity.**

Pruning

Proper pruning is also extremely important for good fruit production. Pruning can be somewhat complicated to understand at first, and many books have been written on how to

❂ Trees should be pruned during the dormant season.

❂ Different tree types require different pruning methods to train the trees properly. Below is a photo showing the training of peaches, apricots, and nectarines.

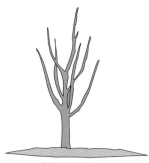

Before pruning

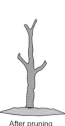

After pruning

prune. As a general rule, the trees should be pruned early each spring, during the dormant season. Prune away any crossing limbs or dead and diseased branches. Proper pruning allows more sunlight to reach the inside branches of the tree.

Each type of tree, however, must be pruned properly in order to train it to grow and be productive. It is important to start training early, if not at planting time, then early the first spring. Two pruning methods are used. Apples, pears, and cherry trees are pruned and trained using the central leader method, consisting of a main, dominant limb and a cone shaped tree. Peaches, nectarines, and apricot trees are pruned and trained in a vase shape. In both instances, pruning is done over a period of time, starting the first year and continuing through the second or third year. After that, all pruning is for maintenance.

Cone-Shaped Central Leader

Starting with a four-foot sapling in the first year, locate the lower scaffold branches, which should be located one and a half to two feet off the ground. Prune out all but five of

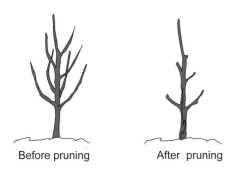

Before pruning   After pruning

⊘ Above shows training apple, pear, plum, and cherry trees.

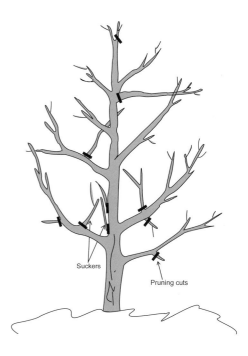

Suckers

Pruning cuts

⊘ Fruit trees also require yearly pruning to keep their shape. Above is a pyramid-shaped tree.

these branches spaced evenly around the trunk. This creates the first scaffold level. Up about one and a half feet above the lower scaffold, prune off all but three more branches, again spaced as evenly as possible around the trunk. Prune back the central leader to create a cone with the two levels of scaffolds. This pruning cut releases growth hormones to the scaffold branches.

For the second-year pruning, prune back each scaffold branch as a separate tree, or cone shape, making the original scaffold branch the central leader of this pruning.

By the third year, the tree should have been trained to its basic shape. All pruning after this point is corrective. Remove all dead and broken branches as well as those that are too low, grow straight up, or those that cross over scaffold branches. Prune away any branches that might block light from the fruiting limbs. Apples form on the inside of the tree.

Vase-Shaped Tree

During the first year choose scaffold branches to form wide angles with the trunk or central leader. The scaffold branches should be about eighteen inches off the ground, but not over thirty-six inches. Trim back the central leader to about one-fourth.

⊗ Above is the pruning for vase-shaped trees.

In the second year, eliminate the central leader completely, thereby creating the vase-shaped tree.

After that, prune the tree regularly. Prune away dead, broken branches or those that have only single-leaf buds and are mostly nonfruiting. Fruiting buds have an outer pair of bud triplets. Keep the middle of the tree thinned so it can get sunlight. Usually after the second year, only light pruning is needed for these trees. One of the biggest problems is the fruiting wood grows farther out on the branch ends. This creates overlong branches that can break when laden with fruit. Keep these branches pruned back yearly.

General Pruning Tips

Always prune back to just in front of the buds aimed in the direction you want the limb to grow. In most instances, these are the buds facing outward, as you want the branches to grow outward rather than inward.

Make your pruning clean using a sharp pruning tool. The cuts should be close to the bud so there is no long stub that won't heal over properly. But

⊗ Metal collars can be used to keep climbing critters away from the fruit.

don't prune too close to damage the bud.

Prune to create wide crotches; narrow crotches will eventually split. Many experts say to prune no closer than at ten and two o'clock angles.

In some instances, you may need to use spreaders on trees to train the branches into more horizontal shapes.

⊗ In seasons with heavy productions you may have to brace up the tree's limbs.

Index

My Garden Plans

My Garden Plans

My Garden Plans

My Garden Plans

My Garden Plans